T0181754

Automated Firewall Analytics

Ehab Al-Shaer

Automated Firewall Analytics

Design, Configuration and Optimization

 Springer

Ehab Al-Shaer
University of North Carolina Charlotte
Charlotte, NC, USA

ISBN 978-3-319-36357-8   ISBN 978-3-319-10371-6 (eBook)
DOI 10.1007/978-3-319-10371-6
Springer Cham Heidelberg New York Dordrecht London

Printed on acid-free paper

Springer is part of Springer Science+Business Media (www.springer.com)

To my wife Ruba and my daughters Abrar, Rawan, Maram, Noor, and Haneen without whom this book would have been completed at least a year ago.

Preface

Firewalls provide the frontier security defense for enterprise networks. Firewalls provide the most critical cybersecurity functions for filtering out unwanted network traffic, which includes attacks and/or unauthorized traffic, coming to or leaving out the secured network. As firewalls on the network border to protect the system from external attacks, they are also used inside the enterprise networks to protect the system from internal attacks by isolating domains of varying security risk levels. In addition, IPSec extends the basic firewall access controls to provide secure communications, providing traffic integrity, confidentiality, and authentication over the Internet.

However, the complexity of managing firewall policies is significant, which limits the effectiveness of firewall security. Typical enterprise networks have hundreds of firewalls and IPSec devices which contain thousands of policy rules. Ad hoc or manual design and configuration management of firewalls is highly subject to human errors. The impact of such complexity has been evidently shown in the increasing number of security vulnerability reports due to operator miscon-figurations. For example, a report from the Center for Strategic and International Studies "Securing Cyberspace for the 44th Presidency" in December 2008 states that "inappropriate or incorrect security configurations were responsible for 80 % of United States Air Force vulnerabilities". A Juniper Networks report "What is Behind Network Downtime?" states that "human errors are blamed for 50–80 % of network outages". Most recent study by Tufin Technologies in 2011 reported that "Nearly 85 % of network administrators in the 2011 Firewall Management report said half of their firewall rule changes need to be fixed because they were configured incorrectly". Thus, managing firewall complexity induces significant impact on budget increase for many enterprises. It has also been stated that "more than 40 % of the total IT budget of a $1 billion-plus company going to human labor and IT operations accounting for 80–90 % of the budget". Moreover, the static rule order in the firewall access control list can cause significant degradation in firewall performance because most-frequently-matched rules could be placed at the end of the policy. Manual reordering based on traffic statistics will be inefficient due to the rapidly changing traffic dynamics.

This book provides a comprehensive and in-depth study for automated firewall policy analysis for designing, configuring, and managing distributed firewalls in large-scale enterpriser networks. The book presents methodologies, techniques, and tools for researchers as well as professionals to understand the challenges and improve the state of the art of managing firewalls systematically in both research and application domains. In Chap. 1, we present techniques based on set theory to automatically detect firewall anomalies (i.e., conflicts) in single or distributed firewalls, and to manage firewall configuration changes globally and consistently. Chapter 2 extends the analysis in Chap. 1 to consider access control list with encryption and authentication such as IPSec polices. This chapter shows the analytical power of modeling firewall and IPSec policies using Binary Decision Diagrams (BDD) to provide compositional verification of conflict-free network access control lists. In Chap. 3, we present a high-level service-oriented firewall configuration language (called FLIP) to enforce firewall security policies globally and correctly in a friendly manner. FLIP allows for defining high-level polices across multiple firewalls in a centralized fashion, which are then translated into access control rules and distributed to the appropriate firewalls with conflict-free guarantees. In Chap. 4, we describe a methodology and framework for designing optimal distributed firewall architecture that minimizes risk while satisfying business connectivity, user usability, and budget constraints. As a result, our presented technique offers a high-level top-down firewall design tool that determines the minimum number, locations, and configurations of firewalls that are required to enforce least-access (or risk) security property while satisfying connectivity, usability, and cost requirements. In each chapter, the book illustrates the concept, algorithm, implementation and case studies and evaluation for each present technique. Chapter 5 presents a practical technique for optimizing firewall performance by reordering firewall rules dynamically based on the real-time traffic statistics, in order to adaptively make the most-frequently-used rules matched first in the access control list. The chapter also presents a taxonomy and comparison of existing dynamic firewall policy configuration techniques based on on-line and off-line traffic analyses.

We would like to acknowledge the contribution of many people to the conception and completion of this book, particulary my colleagues Will Marrero, Radha Jagadeesan, James Riely, and Corin Pitcher for their contributions and comments on the original papers of this book, my students Hazem Hamed and Bin Zhang for their hard work and dedication in their research and running experiments used in this book, and Fadi Mohsen for his editorial help. We gratefully acknowledge NSF, Cisco, and Intel for their in-part support of this work. Finally, we would like to thank my families and our parents for their love and support.

Charlotte, NC, USA   Ehab Al-Shaer
May 2014

Acknowledgements

We gratefully acknowledge NSF, Cisco Systems, and Intel for their funding support of part of this research work.

Contents

Chapter 1
Classification and Discovery of Firewalls Policy Anomalies

Abstract Firewalls are core elements in network security. However, managing firewall rules, particularly in multi-firewall enterprise networks, has become a complex and error-prone task. Firewall filtering rules have to be written, ordered and distributed carefully in order to avoid firewall policy anomalies that might cause network vulnerability. Therefore, inserting or modifying filtering rules in any firewall requires thorough intra- and inter-firewall analysis to determine the proper rule placement and ordering in the firewalls. In this chapter, we identify all anomalies that could exist in a single- or multi-firewall environment. We also present a set of techniques and algorithms to automatically discover policy anomalies in centralized and distributed legacy firewalls. These techniques are implemented in a software tool called the "Firewall Policy Advisor" that simplifies the management of filtering rules and maintains the security of next-generation firewalls.

1.1 Introduction

With the global Internet connection, network security has gained significant attention in research and industrial communities. Due to the increasing threat of network attacks, firewalls have become important elements not only in enterprise networks but also in small-size and home networks. Firewalls have been the frontier defense for secure networks against attacks and unauthorized traffic by filtering out unwanted network traffic coming from or going to the secured network. The filtering decision is based on a set of ordered filtering rules defined according to predefined security policy requirements.

Although deployment of firewall technology is an important step toward securing our networks, the complexity of managing firewall policies might limit the effectiveness of firewall security. In a single firewall environment, the local firewall policy may include *intra-firewall anomalies*, where the same packet may match more than one filtering rule. Moreover, in distributed firewall environments, firewalls might also have *inter-firewall anomalies* when individual firewalls in the same path perform different filtering actions on the same traffic. Therefore, the administrator must give special attention not only to all rule relations in the same firewall in order to determine the correct rule order, but also to all relations between rules in different firewalls in order to determine the proper rule placement in the proper firewall.

© Springer International Publishing Switzerland 2014
E. Al-Shaer, *Automated Firewall Analytics: Design, Configuration and Optimization*, DOI 10.1007/978-3-319-10371-6_1

As the number of filtering rules increases, the difficulty of adding a new rule or modifying an existing one significantly increases. It is very likely, in this case, to introduce conflicting rules such as one general rule shadowing another specific rule, or correlated rules whose relative ordering determines different actions for the same packet. In addition, a typical large-scale enterprise network might involve hundreds of rules that might be written by different administrators in various times. This significantly increases the potential of anomaly occurrence in the firewall policy, jeopardizing the security of the protected network.

Therefore, the effectiveness of firewall security is dependent on providing policy management techniques and tools that network administrators can use to analyze, purify and verify the correctness of written firewall filtering rules. In this chapter, we first provide a formal definition of filtering rule relations and then identify all anomalies that might exist in any firewall policy in both centralized and distributed firewall environments. We also use a tree-based filtering representation to develop anomaly discovery algorithms for reporting any intra- and inter-firewall anomaly in any general network. We finally develop a rule editor to produce anomaly-free firewall policies, and greatly simplify adding, removing and modifying filtering rules. These algorithms and techniques were implemented using Java programming language in a software tool called the "Firewall Policy Advisor".

Although firewall security has been given strong attention in the research community, the emphasis was mostly on the filtering performance issues [6,8,10,11,17]. On the other hand, few related work [7, 10] attempt to address only one of the conflict problems which is the rule correlation in filtering policies. Other approaches [3, 9, 12–14, 18] propose using a high-level policy language to define and analyze firewall policies and then map this language to filtering rules. Although using such high-level languages might avoid rule anomalies, they are not practical for the most widely used firewalls that contain low-level filtering rules. It is simply because redefining already existing policies using high-level languages require far more effort than just analyzing existing rules using stand-alone tools such as the Firewall Policy Advisor. In addition, none of the previous work has a significant attempt to address anomalies in distributed firewalls. Therefore, we consider our work a significant progress in the area as it offers a novel and comprehensive framework to automate anomaly discovery and rule editing in both centralized and distributed legacy firewalls.

This chapter is organized as follows. In Sect. 1.2 we give an introduction to firewall operation. In Sect. 1.3 we present our formalization of filtering rule relations. In Sect. 2.3, we classify and define policy anomalies in centralized firewalls, and then we describe the intra-firewall anomaly discovery algorithm. In Sect. 2.4, we classify and define policy anomalies in distributed firewalls, and then we describe the inter-firewall anomaly discovery algorithm. In Sect. 1.6 we describe the techniques for anomaly-free rule editing. In Sect. 1.7 we show the implementation and evaluation of the Firewall Policy Advisor. Finally, in Sect. 3.5, we show the summary of the chapter (Fig. 1.1).

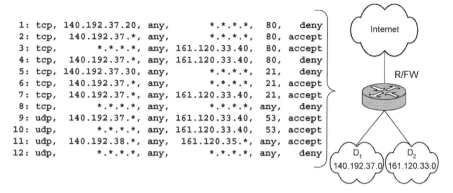

```
 1: tcp,  140.192.37.20, any,        *.*.*.*,   80,   deny
 2: tcp,  140.192.37.*,  any,        *.*.*.*,   80, accept
 3: tcp,        *.*.*.*, any, 161.120.33.40,    80, accept
 4: tcp,  140.192.37.*,  any, 161.120.33.40,    80,   deny
 5: tcp,  140.192.37.30, any,        *.*.*.*,   21,   deny
 6: tcp,  140.192.37.*,  any,        *.*.*.*,   21, accept
 7: tcp,  140.192.37.*,  any, 161.120.33.40,    21, accept
 8: tcp,        *.*.*.*, any,        *.*.*.*,  any,   deny
 9: udp,  140.192.37.*,  any, 161.120.33.40,    53, accept
10: udp,        *.*.*.*, any, 161.120.33.40,    53, accept
11: udp,  140.192.38.*,  any,  161.120.35.*,   any, accept
12: udp,        *.*.*.*, any,        *.*.*.*,  any,   deny
```

Fig. 1.1 An example for centralized firewall setup

1.2 Firewall Background

A firewall is a network element that controls the traversal of packets across the boundaries of a secured network based on a specific security policy. A firewall security policy is a list of ordered filtering rules that define the actions performed on packets that satisfy specific conditions. A rule is composed of set of filtering fields (also called network fields) such as protocol type, source IP address, destination IP address, source port and destination port, as well as an action field. The filtering fields of a rule represent the possible values of the corresponding fields in actual network traffic that matches this rule. Each network field could be a single value or range of values. Filtering actions are either to *accept*, which permits the packet into or from the secure network, or to *deny*, which causes the packet to be blocked. The packet is permitted or blocked by a specific rule if the packet header information matches all the network fields of this rule. Otherwise, the following rule is examined and the process is repeated until a matching rule is found or the default policy action is performed [4, 5]. In this chapter, we assume a "deny" default policy action.

Filtering Rule Format: It is possible to use any field in IP, UDP or TCP headers in the rule filtering part, however, practical experience shows that the most commonly used matching fields are: protocol type, source IP address, source port, destination IP address and destination port [6, 16]. The following is the common format of packet filtering rules in a firewall policy:

```
<order><protocol><s_ip><s_port><d_ip><d_port><action>
```

An example of typical firewall rules is shown in Fig. 5.1.

1.3 Firewall Policy Modelling Using Set Theory

Modelling of firewall rule relations is necessary for analyzing the firewall policy and designing management techniques such as anomaly discovery and policy editing. In this section, we formally describe our model of firewall rule relations.

1.3.1 Formalization of Firewall Rule Relations

To be able to build a useful model for filtering rules, we need to determine all the relations that may relate packet filters. In this section we define all the possible relations that may exist between filtering rules, and we show that there is no other relation exists. We determine the relations based on comparing the network fields of filtering rules as follows.

Definition 1. Rules R_x and R_y are *completely disjoint* if every field in R_x is not a subset nor a superset nor equal to the corresponding field in R_y. Formally, $R_x \Re_{CD} R_y$ iff

$$\forall i : R_x[i] \not\bowtie R_y[i]$$

$$\text{where } \bowtie \in \{\subset, \supset, =\},$$

$$i \in \{\text{protocol, s\_ip, s\_port, d\_ip, d\_port}\}$$

Definition 2. Rules R_x and R_y are *exactly matching* if every field in R_x is equal to the corresponding field in R_y. Formally, $R_x \Re_{EM} R_y$ iff

$$\forall i : R_x[i] = R_y[i]$$

$$\text{where } i \in \{\text{protocol, s\_ip, s\_port, d\_ip, d\_port}\}$$

Definition 3. Rules R_x and R_y are *inclusively matching* if they do not exactly match and if every field in R_x is a subset or equal to the corresponding field in R_y. R_x is called the *subset match* while R_y is called the *superset match*. Formally, $R_x \Re_{IM} R_y$ iff

$$\forall i : R_x[i] \subseteq R_y[i]$$

$$\text{and } \exists j \text{ such that } : R_x[j] \neq R_y[j]$$

$$\text{where } i, j \in \{\text{protocol, s\_ip, s\_port, d\_ip, d\_port}\}$$

For example, in Fig. 5.1, Rule 1 inclusively matches Rule 2. Rule 1 is the subset match of the relation while Rule 2 is the superset match.

Definition 4. Rules R_x and R_y are *partially disjoint* (or *partially matching*) if there is at least one field in R_x that is a subset or a superset or equal to the corresponding field in R_y, and there is at least one field in R_x that is not a subset and not a superset and not equal to the corresponding field in R_y. Formally, $R_x \Re_{PD} R_y$ iff

$$\exists i, j \text{ such that } R_x[i] \bowtie R_y[i] \text{ and } R_x[j] \not\bowtie R_y[j]$$

$$\text{where } \bowtie \, \in \{\subset, \supset, =\},$$

$$i, j \in \{\text{protocol, s\_ip, s\_port, d\_ip, d\_port}\}, i \neq j$$

For example, Rule 2 and Rule 6 in Fig. 5.1 are partially disjoint (or partially matching).

Definition 5. Rules R_x and R_y are *correlated* if some fields in R_x are subsets or equal to the corresponding fields in R_y, and the rest of the fields in R_x are supersets of the corresponding fields in R_y. Formally, $R_x \Re_C R_y$ iff

$$\forall i : R_x[i] \bowtie R_y[i] \text{ and}$$

$$\exists j, k \text{ such that } : R_x[j] \subset R_y[j] \text{ and } R_x[k] \supset R_y[k]$$

$$\text{where } \bowtie \, \in \{\subset, \supset, =\},$$

$$j, k \in \{\text{protocol, s\_ip, s\_port, d\_ip, d\_port}\}, j \neq k$$

For example, Rule 1 and Rule 3 in Fig. 5.1 are correlated.

The following theorems show that these relations are distinct, i.e. only one relation can relate R_x and R_y, and complete, i.e. there is no other relation between R_x and R_y could exist. The complete proofs for the theorems are presented in [1].

Theorem 1. *Any two k-tuple filters in a firewall policy are related by one and only one of the defined relations.*

Theorem 2. *The union of these relations represents the universal set of relations between any two k-tuple filters in a firewall policy.*

1.3.2 Firewall Policy Representation

We represent the firewall policy by a single-rooted tree called the *policy tree* [2]. The tree model provides a simple representation of the filtering rules and at the same time allows for easy discovery of relations and anomalies among these rules. Each node in a policy tree represents a network field, and each branch at this node represents a possible value of the associated field. Every tree path starting at the root

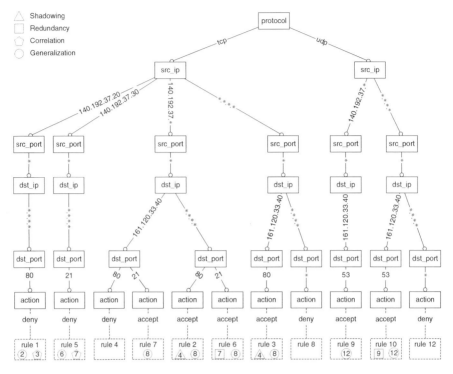

Fig. 1.2 The policy tree for the firewall policy in Fig. 5.1

and ending at a leaf represents a rule in the policy and vice versa. Rules that have the same field value at a specific node will share the same branch representing that value.

Figure 1.2 illustrates the policy tree model of the filtering policy given in Fig. 5.1. Notice that every rule should have an action leaf in the tree. The dotted box below each leaf indicates the rule represented by that branch in addition to other rules that are in anomaly with it as described later in the following section. The tree shows that Rules 1 and 5 each has a separate source address branch as they have different field values, whereas Rules 2, 4, 6 and 7 share the same source address branch as they all have the same field value. Also notice that rule 8 has a separate branch and also appears on other rule branches of which it is a superset, while Rule 4 has a separate branch and also appears on other rule branches of which it is a subset.

1.4 Intra-firewall Anomaly Discovery

The ordering of filtering rules in a centralized firewall policy is very crucial in determining the filtering policy within this firewall. This is because the packet filtering process is performed by sequentially matching the packet against filtering rules until a match is found. If filtering rules are disjoint, the ordering of the rules is insignificant. However, it is very common to have filtering rules that are inter-related. In this case, if the relative rule ordering is not carefully assigned, some rules may be always screened by other rules producing an incorrect policy. Moreover, when the policy contains a large number of filtering rules, the possibility of writing conflicting or redundant rules is relatively high.

An intra-firewall policy anomaly is defined as the existence of two or more filtering rules that may match the same packet or the existence of a rule that can never match any packet on the network paths that cross the firewall [2]. In this section, we classify different anomalies that may exist among filtering rules in one firewall and then describe a technique for discovering these anomalies.

1.4.1   Intra-firewall Anomaly Classification

Here, we describe and then formally define the possible intra-firewall policy anomalies.

1.4.1.1   Shadowing Anomaly

A rule is shadowed when a previous rule matches all the packets that match this rule, such that the shadowed rule will never be activated. Formally, rule R_y is shadowed by rule R_x if:

$$R_x[\text{order}] < R_y[\text{order}], R_x \Re_{\text{EM}} R_y, R_x[\text{action}] \neq R_y[\text{action}]$$
$$R_x[\text{order}] < R_y[\text{order}], R_y \Re_{\text{IM}} R_x, R_x[\text{action}] \neq R_y[\text{action}]$$

For example, Rule 4 in shadowed by Rule 3 in Fig. 5.1. Shadowing is a critical error in the policy, as the shadowed rule never takes effect. This might cause an accepted traffic to be blocked or a denied traffic to be permitted. Therefore, as a general guideline, if there is an inclusive or exact match relationship between two rules, the superset (or general) rule should come after the subset (or specific) rule. It is important to discover shadowed rules and alert the administrator to correct this error by reordering or removing these rules.

1.4.1.2   Correlation Anomaly

Two rules are correlated if they have different filtering actions, and the first rule matches some packets that match the second rule and the second rule matches some packets that match the first rule. Formally, rule R_x and rule R_y have a correlation anomaly if:

$$R_x \Re_C R_y, R_x[\text{action}] \neq R_y[\text{action}]$$

Rule 1 is in correlation with Rule 3 in Fig. 5.1. The two rules with this ordering imply that all HTTP traffic that is coming from 140.192.37.20 and going to 161.120.33.40 is denied. However, if their order is reversed, the same traffic will be accepted. Correlation is considered an anomaly warning because the correlated rules imply an action that is not explicitly stated by the filtering rules. Therefore, in order to resolve this conflict, we point out the correlation between the rules and prompt the user to choose the proper order that complies with the security policy requirements.

1.4.1.3 Generalization Anomaly

A rule is a generalization of a preceding rule if they have different actions, and if the first rule can match all the packets that match the second rule. Formally, rule R_y is a generalization of rule R_x if:

$$R_x[\text{order}] < R_y[\text{order}], R_x \Re_{IM} R_y, R_x[\text{action}] \neq R_y[\text{action}]$$

Rule 2 is a generalization of Rule 1 in Fig. 5.1. These two rules imply that all HTTP traffic that is coming from the address 140.192.37.* will be accepted, except the traffic coming from 140.192.37.20. Generalization is often used to exclude a specific part of the traffic from a general filtering action. It is considered only an anomaly warning because the specific rule makes an exception of the general rule. This might cause an accepted traffic to be blocked or a denied traffic to be permitted, and thus it is important to highlight its action to the administrator for confirmation.

1.4.1.4 Redundancy Anomaly

A redundant rule performs the same action on the same packets as another rule such that if the redundant rule is removed, the security policy will not be affected. Formally, rule R_y is redundant to rule R_x if:

$$R_x[\text{order}] < R_y[\text{order}], R_x \Re_{EM} R_y, R_x[\text{action}] = R_y[\text{action}]$$
$$R_x[\text{order}] < R_y[\text{order}], R_y \Re_{IM} R_x, R_x[\text{action}] = R_y[\text{action}]$$

Whereas rule R_x is redundant to rule R_y if:

$$R_x[\text{order}] < R_y[\text{order}], R_x \Re_{IM} R_y, R_x[\text{action}] = R_y[\text{action}]$$

and $\not\exists R_z$ where $R_x[\text{order}] < R_z[\text{order}] < R_y[\text{order}]$,

$$R_x\{\mathfrak{R}_{IM}, \mathfrak{R}_C\}R_z, R_x[\text{action}] \neq R_z[\text{action}]$$

Referring to Fig. 5.1, Rule 7 is redundant to Rule 6, and Rule 9 is redundant to Rule 10. Redundancy is considered an error in the firewall policy because a redundant rule adds to the size of the filtering rule list, and therefore increases the search time and space requirements of the packet filtering process [15]. In general, to avoid redundant rules, a superset rule following a subset rule should have an opposite filtering action. It is important to discover redundant rules so that the administrator may modify the filtering action or remove the rules from the policy.

1.4.1.5 Irrelevance Anomaly

A filtering rule in a firewall is irrelevant if this rule cannot match any traffic that might flow through this firewall. This exists when both the source address and the destination address fields of the rule do not match any domain reachable through this firewall. In other words, the path between the source and destination addresses of this rule does not pass through the firewall. Thus, this rule has no effect on the filtering outcome of this firewall. Formally, rule R_x in firewall F is irrelevant if:

$$F \notin \{n : n \text{ is a node on a path from } R_x[\text{src}] \text{ to } R_x[\text{dst}]\}$$

Referring to Fig. 5.1, Rule 11 is irrelevant because the traffic that goes between the source (140.192.38.*) and the destination (161.120.35.*) does not pass through this firewall.

Irrelevance is considered an anomaly because it adds unnecessary overhead to the filtering process and it does not contribute to the policy semantics. It is well-understood that keeping the filtering rule table as small as possible helps in improving the overall firewall performance [15, 16]. Thus, discovering irrelevant rules is an important function for the network security administrator.

1.4.2 Intra-firewall Anomaly Discovery Algorithm

The state diagram in Fig. 1.3 illustrates intra-firewall anomaly discovery states for any two rules, R_x and R_y, where the two rules are in the same firewall and R_y follows R_x. For simplicity, the address and port fields are integrated in one field for both the source and destination. This reduces the number of states and simplifies the explanation of the diagram.

Initially no relationship is assumed. Each field in R_y is compared to the corresponding field in R_x starting with the protocol, then source address and port, and finally destination address and port. The relationship between the two rules is

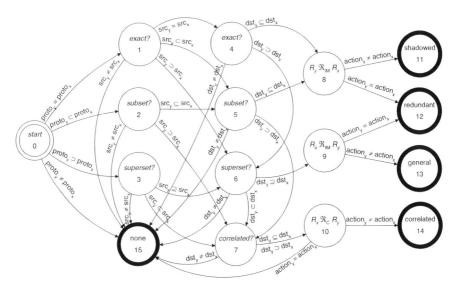

Fig. 1.3 State diagram for detecting intra-firewall anomalies for rules R_x and R_y, where R_y comes after R_x

determined based on the result of subsequent comparisons. If every field of R_y is a subset or equal to the corresponding field in R_x and both rules have the same action, R_y is redundant to R_x, while if the actions are different, R_y is shadowed by R_x. If every field of R_y is a superset or equal to the corresponding field in R_x and both rules have the same action, R_x is potentially redundant to R_y, while if the actions are different, R_y is a generalization of R_x. If some fields of R_x are subsets or equal to the corresponding fields in R_y, and some fields of R_x are supersets to the corresponding fields in R_y, and their actions are different, then R_x is in correlation with R_y. Identifying irrelevant rules requires the knowledge of the network connectivity. Discovering this intra-firewall anomaly is discussed later in Sect. 1.5.3 along with the inter-firewall anomaly discovery algorithm. If none of the preceding cases occur, then the two rules do not involve any anomalies.

The basic idea for discovering anomalies is to determine if any two rules coincide in their policy tree paths. If the path of a rule coincides with the path of another rule, there is a potential anomaly that can be determined based on intra-firewall anomaly definitions in Sect. 1.4.1. If rule paths do not coincide, then these rules are disjoint and they have no anomalies. The detailed description of the intra-firewall anomaly discovery algorithm is available in [1]. Applying the algorithm on the rules in Fig. 5.1, the discovered anomalies are marked in the dotted boxes at the bottom of the policy tree in Fig. 1.2. Shadowed rules are marked with a triangle, redundant rules with a square, correlated rules with a pentagon and generalization rules with a circle.

1.5 Inter-firewall Anomaly Discovery

It is very common to have multiple firewalls installed in the same enterprise network. This has many network administration advantages. It gives local control for each domain according to the domain security requirements and applications. For example, some domains might demand to block RTSP traffic or multicast traffic, however, other domains in the same network might request to receive the same traffic. Multi-firewall installation also provides inter-domain security, and protection from internally generated traffic. Moreover, end-users might use firewalls in their personal workstations for other reasons. However, because of the decentralized nature inherent to the security policy in distributed firewalls, the potential of anomalies between firewalls significantly increases. Even if every firewall policy in the network does not contain rule anomalies described in Sect. 1.4.1, there could be anomalies between policies of different firewalls. For example, an upstream firewall might block a traffic that is permitted by a downstream firewall or vice versa. In the first case, this anomaly is called inter-firewall "shadowing" which similar in principle to rule shadowing discussed in the intra-firewall anomaly analysis. In the other case, the resulted anomaly is called "spurious traffic" because it allows unwanted traffic to cross portions of the network and increases the network vulnerability to denial of service attack. In this section, we first define the anomalies that may exist in a distributed firewall environment, and then we identify with examples different types of inter-firewall anomalies and we describe a technique to discover these anomalies.

1.5.1 Inter-firewall Anomaly Definition

In general, an inter-firewall anomaly may exist if any two firewalls on a network path take different filtering actions on the same traffic. We first illustrate the simple case of multiple cascaded firewalls isolating two network sub-domains where the firewalls are installed at the routing points in the network.

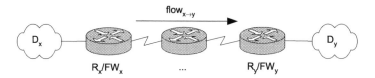

Fig. 1.4 Cascaded firewalls isolating domains D_x and D_y

Referring to Fig. 1.4, we assume a traffic stream flowing from sub-domain D_x to sub-domain D_y across multiple cascaded firewalls installed on the network path between the two sub-domains. At any point on this path in the direction of flow, a preceding firewall is called an *upstream firewall* whereas a following firewall is

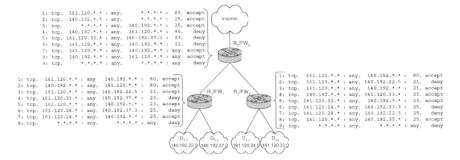

Fig. 1.5 An example for a hierarchical distributed firewall setup

called a *downstream firewall*. The closest firewall to the flow source sub-domain (FW_x) is called the *most-upstream firewall*, while The closest firewall to the flow destination sub-domain (FW_y) is called the *most-downstream firewall*.

Using the above network model, we can say that for any traffic flowing from sub-domain D_x to sub-domain D_y an anomaly exists if one of the following conditions holds:

1. The most-downstream firewall accepts a traffic that is blocked by any of the upstream firewalls.
2. The most-upstream firewall permits a traffic that is blocked by any of the downstream firewalls.
3. A downstream firewall denies a traffic that is already blocked by the most-upstream firewall.

On the other hand, all upstream firewalls should permit any traffic that is permitted by the most-downstream firewall in order that the flow can reach the destination.

1.5.2   Inter-firewall Anomaly Classification

In this section, we classify anomalies in multi-firewall environments. Our classification rules are based on the basic case of cascaded firewalls illustrated in Fig. 1.4, assuming the network traffic is flowing from domain D_x to domain D_y. Rule R_u belongs to the policy of the most-upstream firewall FW_x, while rule R_d belongs to the policy of the most-downstream firewall FW_y. We assume that no intra-firewall shadowing or redundancy exists in any individual firewall. As illustrated in Sect. 1.4.1, this implies that every "deny" rule should be followed by a more general "accept" rule, and the default action of unspecified traffic is "deny".

1.5.2.1 Shadowing Anomaly

A shadowing anomaly occurs if an upstream firewall blocks the network traffic accepted by a downstream firewall. Formally, rule R_d is shadowed by rule R_u if one of the following conditions holds:

$$R_d \mathfrak{R}_{EM} R_u, R_u[\text{action}]=\text{deny}, R_d[\text{action}]=\text{accept} \tag{1.1}$$

$$R_d \mathfrak{R}_{IM} R_u, R_u[\text{action}]=\text{deny}, R_d[\text{action}]=\text{accept} \tag{1.2}$$

$$R_u \mathfrak{R}_{IM} R_d, R_u[\text{action}]=\text{deny}, R_d[\text{action}]=\text{accept} \tag{1.3}$$

$$R_u \mathfrak{R}_{IM} R_d, R_u[\text{action}]=\text{accept}, R_d[\text{action}]=\text{accept} \tag{1.4}$$

Intuitively, in cases (1.1) and (1.2), the upstream firewall completely blocks the traffic permitted by the downstream firewall. Rules $(2/FW_2, 3/FW_1)$, and Rules $(8/FW_1, 4/FW_2)$ in Fig. 1.5 are examples of cases (1.1) and (1.2) respectively. In cases (1.3) and (1.4) the upstream firewall partially blocks the traffic permitted by the downstream firewall. Rules $(7/FW_2, 7/FW_1)$, and Rules $(5/FW_2, 5/FW_1)$ in Fig. 1.5 are examples of cases (1.3) and (1.4) respectively.

1.5.2.2 Spuriousness Anomaly

A spuriousness anomaly occurs if an upstream firewall permits the network traffic denied by a downstream firewall. Formally, rule R_u allows spurious traffic to rule R_d if one of the following conditions holds:

$$R_u \mathfrak{R}_{EM} R_d, R_u[\text{action}]=\text{accept}, R_d[\text{action}]=\text{deny} \tag{1.5}$$

$$R_u \mathfrak{R}_{IM} R_d, R_u[\text{action}]=\text{accept}, R_d[\text{action}]=\text{deny} \tag{1.6}$$

$$R_d \mathfrak{R}_{IM} R_u, R_u[\text{action}]=\text{accept}, R_d[\text{action}]=\text{deny} \tag{1.7}$$

$$R_d \mathfrak{R}_{IM} R_u, R_u[\text{action}]=\text{accept}, R_d[\text{action}]=\text{accept} \tag{1.8}$$

$$R_u \mathfrak{R}_{IM} R_d, R_u[\text{action}]=\text{deny}, R_d[\text{action}]=\text{deny} \tag{1.9}$$

In cases (1.5) and (1.6), the rule R_u in the upstream firewall permits unwanted traffic because it is completely blocked by R_d in the downstream firewall. Examples of these cases are Rules $(2/FW_1, 4/FW_0)$, and Rules $(2/FW_1, 9/FW_2)$ in Fig. 1.5 respectively. In cases (1.7) and (1.8) part of the traffic allowed by rule R_u in upstream firewall is undesired spurious traffic since it is blocked by rule R_d in the downstream firewall. Examples of these cases are also found in Rules $(5/FW_2, 4/FW_1)$, and $(3/FW_2, 3/FW_1)$ in Fig. 1.5 respectively. Case (1.9) is not as obvious as the previous cases and it needs further analysis. Since we assume there is no intra-firewall redundancy in the upstream firewall, the fact that R_u has a "deny" action implies that there exists a superset rule in the upstream firewall that follows R_u and accepts some traffic blocked by R_d. This occurs when the implied "accept" rule in the upstream firewall is an exact, superset or subset match (but not correlated) of R_d. Rules ($5/FW_0$, $4/FW_1$) in Fig. 1.5 are an example of this case.

1.5.2.3   Redundancy Anomaly

A redundancy anomaly occurs if a downstream firewall denies the network traffic already blocked by an upstream firewall. Formally, rule R_d is redundant to rule R_u if, on every path to which R_u and R_d are relevant, one of the following conditions holds:

$$R_d \Re_{EM} R_u, R_u[\text{action}]=\text{deny}, R_d[\text{action}]=\text{deny} \qquad (1.10)$$

$$R_d \Re_{IM} R_u, R_u[\text{action}]=\text{deny}, R_d[\text{action}]=\text{deny} \qquad (1.11)$$

In both of these cases, the deny action in the downstream firewall is unnecessary because all the traffic denied by R_d is already blocked by R_u in the upstream firewall. In Fig. 1.5, Rules ($6/FW_2$, $6/FW_1$), and Rules ($9/FW_2$, $6/FW_0$) are examples of cases (1.10) and (1.11) respectively.

1.5.2.4   Correlation Anomaly

A correlation anomaly occurs as a result of having two correlated rules in the upstream and downstream firewalls. We defined correlated rules in Sect. 1.3.1. Intra-firewall correlated rules have an anomaly only if these rules have different filtering actions. However, correlated rules having any action are always a source of anomaly in distributed firewalls because of the implied rule resulting from the conjunction of the correlated rules. This creates not only ambiguity in the inter-firewall policy, but also spurious, and shadowing anomalies. Formally, the correlation anomaly for rules R_u and R_d occurs if one of the following conditions holds:

$$R_u \Re_C R_d, R_u[\text{action}]=\text{accept}, R_d[\text{action}]=\text{accept} \qquad (1.12)$$

$$R_u \Re_C R_d, R_u[\text{action}]=\text{deny}, R_d[\text{action}]=\text{deny} \qquad (1.13)$$

$$R_u \Re_C R_d, R_u[\text{action}]=\text{accept}, R_d[\text{action}]=\text{deny} \qquad (1.14)$$

$$R_u \Re_C R_d, R_u[\text{action}]=\text{deny}, R_d[\text{action}]=\text{accept} \qquad (1.15)$$

An example for case (1.12) is
$R_u : \text{tcp}, 140.192.*.*, \text{any}, 161.120.33.*, 80, \text{accept}$
$R_d : \text{tcp}, 140.192.37.*, \text{any}, 161.120.*.*, 80, \text{accept}$
In this example, effectively, the correlative conjunction of these two rules implies that only the traffic coming from 140.192.37.* and destined to 161.120.33.*. will be accepted as indicated in the following implied rule R_i

R_i : tcp, 140.192.37.*, any, 161.120.33.*, 80, accept
This means that other traffic destined to 161.120.*.* will be shadowed at the upstream firewall, while spurious traffic originating from 140.192.*.* will reach the downstream firewall.

For case (1.13) the example is

R_u : tcp, 140.192. *.*, any, 161.120.33.*, 80, deny

R_d : tcp, 140.192.37.*, any, 161.120. *.*, 80, deny

In this case, the resulting action at the downstream firewall will deny the traffic coming from 140.192.37.* and destined to 161.120.33.*. The implied filtering rule R_i will be

R_i : tcp, 140.192.37.*, any, 161.120.33.*, 80, deny
This means that other traffic originating from 140.192.*.* will be shadowed at the upstream firewall, while spurious traffic destined to 161.120.*.* may reach the downstream firewall. A possible resolution for cases (1.12) and (1.13) is to replace each of the correlated rules with the implied filtering rule R_i.

The example for case (1.14) is

R_u : tcp, 140.192. *.*, any, 161.120.33.*, 80, accept

R_d : tcp, 140.192.37.*, any, 161.120. *.*, 80,   deny

This example shows that the resulting filtering action at the upstream firewall permits the traffic that is coming from 140.192.37.* and destined to 161.120.33.*. However, the same traffic is blocked at the downstream firewall, resulting in spurious traffic flow. To resolve this anomaly, an extra rule R_i should be added in the upstream firewall prior to R_u such that it blocks the spurious traffic as follows

R_i : tcp, 140.192.37.*, any, 161.120.33.*, 80,   deny

As for case (1.15), the example is

R_u : tcp, 140.192. *.*, any, 161.120.33.*, 80,   deny

R_d : tcp, 140.192.37.*, any, 161.120. *.*, 80, accept

This example shows a different situation where the resulting filtering action at the upstream firewall will block the traffic that is coming from 140.192.37.* and destined to 161.120.33.*. However, because this traffic is accepted at the downstream firewall, R_d is shadowed by R_u. To resolve this anomaly, an extra rule R_i should be added in the upstream firewall before R_u to avoid the shadowing anomaly as follows

R_i : tcp, 140.192.37.*, any, 161.120.33.*, 80, accept

In the following theorem, we show that the anomaly cases we presented above are covering all the possible inter-firewall anomalies. A complete proof of the theorem is provided in [1].

Theorem 3. *This set of anomalies represent all filtering anomalies that might exist between any two rules each in a different firewall.*

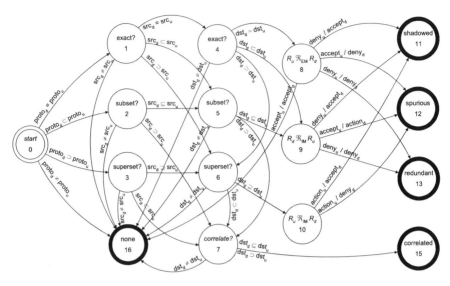

Fig. 1.6 State diagram for inter-firewall anomaly discovery for rules R_u and R_d, where R_u belongs to the upstream firewall and R_d belongs to the downstream firewall

1.5.3   Inter-firewall Anomaly Discovery Algorithm

This algorithm finds the rule relations described in Sect. 1.5.2 and discovers the anomalies between filtering rules in two or more connected firewalls. In Fig. 1.6 we show the state diagram of the inter-firewall anomaly discovery algorithm. The figure shows the anomaly discovery for any two rules, R_u and R_d, where R_u is a rule in the upstream firewall policy, and R_d is a rule in the downstream firewall policy. For simplicity, the address and port fields are integrated in one field for both the source and destination. At the start state, we assume no relationship between the two rules. Each field in R_d is compared to the corresponding field in R_u starting with the protocol then source and destination addresses and ports. Based on these comparisons, the relation between the two rules is determined, as well as the anomaly if it exists. For example, if R_u is found to inclusively match R_d (State 10), then R_d is partially shadowed if its action is "accept" (State 11), or R_u is spurious if the action of R_d is "deny" (State 12).

Since more than two firewalls may exist between sub-domains in an enterprise network, the inter-firewall anomaly discovery process should be performed on all firewalls in the path connecting any two sub-domains in the network. For example, in Fig. 1.5, inter-firewall anomaly analysis is performed on (FW_1, FW_0) for all traffic that goes between $D_{1.2}$ and the Internet, on (FW_2, FW_0) for all traffic that goes between $D_{2.2}$ and the Internet, and on (FW_1, FW_0, FW_2) for all traffic that goes between $D_{1.2}$ and $D_{2.2}$. Although we use a hierarchical network topology example, this analysis can be performed on any network topology as long as there is a fixed route between source and destination sub-domains.

Intuitively, inter-firewall anomaly discovery is performed by aggregating the policy trees presented in Sect. 1.3.2 for all the firewalls isolating every two sub-domains in the network. The algorithm takes as an input the list of network paths between sub-domains. For each path, we determine all the firewalls in the traffic flow. Then for every firewall in the path, we first run the intra-firewall anomaly discovery algorithm described in Sect. 1.4.2 to ensure that every individual firewall is free from intra-firewall anomalies. Next, we build the policy tree of the most upstream firewall and then add into this tree the rules of all the consecutive firewalls in the path. During this process, only the rules that apply to this path (have the same source and destination) are selected and marked. Eventually, as a result of applying the algorithm on all the network paths, the rules that potentially create anomalies are reported. In addition, any rule left unmarked is reported as an irrelevant rule anomaly as it does not apply to any path in the network. The complete description of the inter-firewall anomaly discovery algorithm is provided in [1].

As an example, we apply the inter-firewall anomaly discovery algorithm on the example network in Fig. 1.5. We start by identifying the participating sub-domains in the network given the network topology and routing tables. The domains in the figure are $D_{1.1}$, $D_{1.2}$, $D_{2.1}$, $D_{2.2}$ in addition to the global Internet domain. The Internet domain is basically any address that does not belong to one of the network sub-domains. Afterwards, we identify all the possible directed paths between any two sub-domains in the network and determine the firewalls that control the traffic on that path, and we run the algorithm on each one of these paths. According to the figure, the algorithm analyzes 20 distinct paths for inter-firewall anomalies and produces the anomalies indicated in Sect. 1.5.2.

1.6 Anomaly-Free Firewall Policy Editing

Firewall policies are often written by different network administrators and occasionally updated (by inserting, modifying or removing rules) to accommodate new security requirements and network topology changes. Editing an enterprise security policy can be far more difficult than creating a new one. A new filtering rule may not apply to every network sub-domain, therefore this rule should be properly located in the correct firewalls to avoid blocking or permitting the wrong traffic. Moreover, as rules in a local firewall policy are ordered, a new rule must be inserted in a particular order to avoid creating intra-firewall anomalies. The same applies if the rule is modified or removed. In this section, we present firewall policy editing techniques that simplify the rule editing task significantly, and avoids introducing anomalies due to policy updates. The policy editor helps the user to determine the correct firewalls at which a new rule should be located avoiding inter-firewall anomalies, and helps to determine the proper order for the rule within these firewalls avoiding intra-firewall anomalies, and provides visual aids for users to track and verify policy changes. Using the policy editor, administrators require no prior knowledge or understating of the firewall policy in order to insert, modify or remove a rule.

1.6.1 Rule Insertion

The process of inserting a new rule in the global security policy is performed in two steps. The first step is to identify the firewalls in which this rule should be deployed. This is needed in order to apply the filtering rule only on the relevant sub-domains without creating any inter-firewall anomalies. The second step is to determine the proper order of the rule in each firewall so that no intra-firewall anomaly is created.

In the first step, we first identify all the possible paths that go from the source address to the destination address of the rule. If any of the source or destination addresses is an external address (Internet address), then we find the path to/from the closest firewall to the Internet. Second, the rule is inserted in all firewalls in the identified paths if the rule action is "accept." Otherwise, the rule is inserted only in the most-upstream firewalls(s) relative to the source(s). As an example, the following two rules are inserted in the security policy shown in Fig. 1.5:

R_1 : icmp, $*.*.*.*$, any, $140.192.*.*$, any, deny

R_2 : icmp, $140.192.*.*$, any, $161.120.*.*$, any, accept

R_1 is installed in firewalls FW_0 and FW_2 because they are the most-upstream firewalls on the paths from the Internet and domain D_2 ($161.120.*.*$) to domain D_1 ($140.192.*.*$) respectively. On the other hand, R_2 is installed in firewalls FW_0, FW_1 and FW_2 because they all exist on the path from the domain D_1 ($140.192.*.*$) to domain D_2 ($161.120.*.*$).

In the second step, the order of the new rule in the local firewall policy is determined based on its relation with other existing rules. In general, a new rule should be inserted before any rule that is a superset match, and after any rule that is a subset match of this rule. The local policy tree is used to keep track of the correct ordering of the new rule, and discover any potential anomalies. We start by searching for the correct rule position in the policy tree by comparing the fields of the new rule with the corresponding tree branch values. If the field value is a subset of the branch, then the order of the new rule so far is smaller than the minimum order of all the rules in this branch. If the field value is a superset of the branch, the order of the new rule so far is greater than the maximum order of all the rules in this branch. On the other hand, if the rule is disjoint, then it can given any order in the policy. Similarly, the tree browsing continues evaluating the next fields in the rule recursively as long as the field value is an exact match or a subset match of a branch. When the action field is reached, the rule is inserted and assigned an order within the maximum and minimum range determined in the browsing phase. A new branch is created for the new rule any time a disjoint or superset match is found. If the new rule is redundant because it is an exact match or a subset match and it has the same action of an existing rule, the policy editor rejects it and prompts the user with an appropriate message.

After inserting the rule in the appropriate firewalls, the inter-firewall anomaly discovery algorithm in Sect. 1.5.3 is activated to verify that no intra-firewall or inter-firewall anomalies are introduced in the distributed security policy, and to identify any correlation or generalization anomalies the new rule might have created.

1.6.2 Rule Removal

In distributed firewall environments, removing a rule from a specific firewall may result in creating an inter-firewall anomaly. For example, if a "deny" rule is removed from the upstream firewall, this may result in spurious traffic flowing downstream, but if an "accept" rule is removed from the upstream firewall, the relevant traffic may be blocked and all the related (exact, subset or superset) downstream rules will be shadowed.

When the user decides to remove a rule from a certain firewall, the first step is to identify all the source and destination sub-domains that will be impacted by removing this rule. We use the same technique described in rule insertion process to determine the network path between every source-destination domain pair relevant to this rule. In the second step, we remove the rule from the firewall policy as follows. If the rule is an "accept" rule, then we remove it from the firewalls in all paths from source to destination. Otherwise, shadowing and/or spuriousness anomaly is created if the rule is removed from the upstream and/or the downstream firewalls respectively. However, if the rule is a "deny" rule, then we just remove it from the local firewall and alert the administrator of the extra traffic that will be permitted as a result of removing this rule. After removing the rule, we run the inter-firewall anomaly analysis in order to highlight any potential anomalies that might be introduced in the modified policy.

Modifying a rule in a firewall policy is also a critical operation. However, a modified rule can be easily verified and inserted based on the rule removal and insertion techniques described above.

1.7 Firewall Policy Advisor: Implementation and Evaluation

We implemented the techniques and algorithms described in Sects. 2.4 and 2.3 in a software tool called the "Firewall Policy Advisor" or FPA. The tool implements the inter-firewall and intra-firewall anomaly discovery algorithms, as well as the distributed firewall policy editor. The FPA was developed using Java programming language and it includes a graphical user interface. In this section, we present our evaluation study of the usability and the performance of the anomaly discovery techniques described in this chapter (Fig. 1.7).

To assess the practical value of our techniques, we first used the FPA tool to analyze real firewall rules in our university network as well as in some local industrial networks in the area. In many cases, the FPA has shown to be effective by discovering many firewall anomalies that were not discovered by human visual inspection. We then attempted to quantitatively evaluate the practical usability of the FPA by conducting a set of experiments that consider the level of network administrator expertise and the frequency of occurrence of each anomaly type. In this experiment, we created two firewall policy exercises and asked 12 network

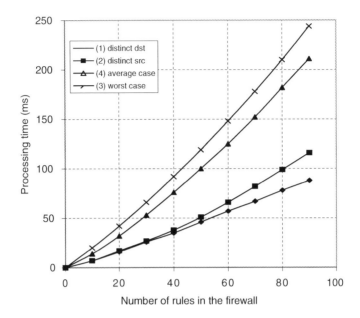

Fig. 1.7 Processing time for intra-firewall anomaly discovery

Table 1.1 The average percentage of discovered anomalies in a man-written centralized firewall policy

Experience	Shadowing (%)	Redundancy (%)	Correlation (%)	Irrelevance (%)
Expert	0	5	3	0
Intermediate	1	9	3	0
Beginner	4	12	9	2

Table 1.2 The average percentage of discovered anomalies in a man-written distributed firewall policy

Experience	Shadowing (%)	Spuriousness (%)	Redundancy (%)	Correlation (%)
Expert	1	7	9	1
Intermediate	3	10	11	2
Beginner	6	14	17	2

administrators with varying level of expertise in the field to complete each exercise. The exercises include writing filtering rules in centralized and distributed firewalls based on a given security policy requirements. We then used the FPA tool to analyze the rules in the answer of each one and calculated the ratio of each anomaly relative to total number of rules. The average total number of rules was 40 in the centralized firewall, and 90 in the distributed firewall for a network having only three firewalls. The results of this experiment are shown in Tables 1.1 and 1.2 for the centralized and distributed firewall exercises respectively.

These results show clearly that the margin of error that can be done even by an expert administrator is quite significant (about 8 % for centralized one and 18 % for the distributed one). This figure is even much higher for an intermediate and beginner administrators (about 13 % and 27 % for centralized firewall and 26 % and 39 % for the distritbuted firewalls respectively). Another interesting observation is the high percentage of redundant as well as spurious rules in all experience levels.

In the last phase of our evaluation study, we conducted number of experiments to measure the performance and the scalability of firewall anomaly discovery under different filtering policies and network topologies. Our experiments were performed on a Pentium PIII 400 MHz processor with 128 MB of RAM.

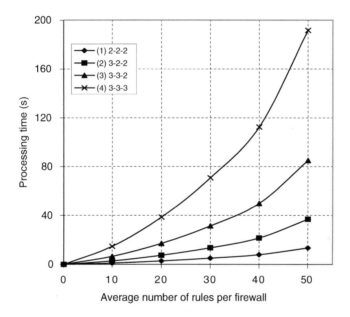

Fig. 1.8 Processing time for inter-firewall anomaly discovery

To study the performance of the intra-firewall anomaly discovery algorithm, we produced four sets of firewall rules. The first set includes rules that are different in the destination address only, and the second set includes rules that have distinct source addresses. These two sets resemble a realistic combination of practical firewall rules, and represent the best case scenario because they require the minimum policy-tree navigation for analyzing each rule. In the third set, each rule is a superset match of the preceding rule. This set represents the worst case scenario because each rule requires complete policy-tree navigation in order to analyze the entire rule set. The fourth set includes rules that are randomly selected from the three previous sets in order to represent the average case scenario. We used the FPA tool to run the intra-firewall policy analysis algorithm on each set using various sizes of rule sets (10–90 rules). In each case, we measured the processing time needed to produce the policy analysis report. The results we obtained are shown in Fig. 2.8. Set 1 shows the least processing time because all the rules are aggregated in one branch in the policy tree, which makes the number of field matches and node creations minimal. Set 2 has a slightly higher processing time, since each rule in the set has a distinct branch at a higher level in the policy tree. This requires more time to create new tree nodes for inserting each rule in the tree. Set 3 is expected to have the highest processing time since every rule in the set must be matched with all rules in the policy tree. Set 4 shows a moderate (average) processing time and represents the most practical scenario as it combines many different cases. Even in the worst case scenario (Set 3), the processing time looks very reasonable; approximately 20–240 ms for 10–90 rules. In addition, the processing time increases about 2.1–2.8 ms per rule, which is considered insignificant overhead even if hundreds of rules exist in a firewall.

For evaluating the performance of the inter-firewall anomaly discovery algorithm, we conducted a similar experiment on a network of distributed firewalls. We used a balanced three-level hierarchical network topology connected to the Internet via the root node. Each non-leaf node in the network has filtering capability. We created four networks with different branching degrees at each level in the hierarchy starting at the root node: (1) 2-2-2, (2) 3-2-2, (3) 3-3-2 and (4) 3-3-3. For example, the root node in Network 2 has three branches, whereas every node on levels two and three has two branches. For each network, we installed a random set of filtering rules in each firewall. The generated topology information and the firewall setup of each network are used as inputs for our experiment. We then used the FPA to run the inter-firewall policy analysis algorithm on each network with a different number of rules (10–50 rules) for each firewall. We measured, in each case, the processing time required to produce the final policy analysis report. The results are shown in Fig. 1.8. We noticed that for small and mid-size networks (such as Network 1 that has 8 sub-domains and Network 2 that has 12 sub-domains), the processing time ranges from 3 to 40 s. However, in case of large networks (such as Networks 3 and Network 4 that have 18 and 27 sub-domains respectively), the firewall anomaly discovery requires much higher processing time ranging from 11 to 180 s depending on the rule complexity. The increase in the processing time as the network size increases is due to the fact that the complexity of our algorithm is dependant on the total number of paths between sub-domains in the network.

1.8 Summary

Firewall security, like any other technology, requires proper management in order to provide proper security services. Thus, just having firewalls on the network boundaries or between sub-domains may not necessarily make the network any secure. One reason of this is the complexity of managing firewall rules and the resulting network vulnerability due to rule anomalies. The Firewall Policy Advisor presented in this chapter provides a number of techniques for purifying and protecting the firewall policy from rule anomalies. The administrator may use the firewall policy advisor to manage legacy firewall policies without prior analysis of filtering rules. In this chapter, we formally defined a number of firewall policy anomalies in both centralized and distributed firewalls and we proved that these are the only conflicts that could exist in firewall policies. We then presented a set of algorithms to detect rule anomalies within a single firewall (intra-firewall anomalies), and between inter-connected firewalls (inter-firewall anomalies) in the network. When an anomaly is detected, users are prompted with proper corrective actions. We intentionally made the tool not to automatically correct the discovered anomaly but rather alarm the user because we believe that the administrator should have the final call on policy changes. Finally, we presented a user-friendly Java-based implementation of Firewall Policy Advisor.

Using Firewall Policy Advisor was shown to be very effective for firewalls in real-life networks. In regards to usability, the tool was able to discover filtering anomalies in rules written by expert network administrators. In regards to performance, although the policy analysis algorithms are parabolically dependant on the number of rules in the firewall policy, our experiments show that the average processing time in intra- and inter-firewall anomaly discovery is very reasonable for practical applications. Using our Java implementation of the anomaly discovery algorithms, our results indicate that it, in the worst case, it takes 10–240 ms of processing time to analyze a security policy of 10–90 rules in a single firewall. However, in a considerably large network (27 sub-domains with 13 firewalls), it takes 20–180 s to analyze the filtering rules of all firewalls in the network.

References

1. E. Al-Shaer and H. Hamed. "Design and Implementation of Firewall Policy Advisor Tools." *DePaul CTI Technical Report, CTI-TR-02-006*, August 2002.
2. E. Al-Shaer and H. Hamed. "Firewall Policy Advisor for Anomaly Detection and Rule Editing." *IEEE/IFIP Integrated Management Conference (IM'2003)*, March 2003.
3. Y. Bartal., A. Mayer, K. Nissim and A. Wool. "Firmato: A Novel Firewall Management Toolkit." *Proceedings of 1999 IEEE Symposium on Security and Privacy*, May 1999.
4. D. Chapman and E. Zwicky. *Building Internet Firewalls, Second Edition*, Orielly & Associates Inc., 2000.
5. W. Cheswick and S. Belovin. *Firewalls and Internet Security*, Addison-Wesley, 1995.
6. S. Cobb. "ICSA Firewall Policy Guide v2.0." NCSA Security White Paper Series, 1997.
7. D. Eppstein and S. Muthukrishnan. "Internet Packet Filter Management and Rectangle Geometry." *Proceedings of 12th Annual ACM-SIAM Symposium on Discrete Algorithms (SODA)*, January 2001.
8. Z. Fu, F. Wu, H. Huang, K. Loh, F. Gong, I. Baldine and C. Xu. "IPSec/VPN Security Policy: Correctness, Conflict Detection and Resolution." *Proceedings of Policy'2001 Workshop*, January 2001.
9. J. Guttman. "Filtering Posture: Local Enforcement for Global Policies." *Proceedings of 1997 IEEE Symposium on security and Privacy*, May 1997.
10. B. Hari, S. Suri and G. Parulkar. "Detecting and Resolving Packet Filter Conflicts." *Proceedings of IEEE INFOCOM'00*, March 2000.

11. S. Hazelhusrt. "Algorithms for Analyzing Firewall and Router Access Lists." *Technical Report TR-WitsCS-1999*, Department of Computer Science, University of the Witwatersrand, South Africa, July 1999.
12. S. Hinrichs. "Policy-Based Management: Bridging the Gap." *Proceedings of 15th Annual Computer Security Applications Conference (ACSAC'99)*, December 1999.
13. E. Lupu and M. Sloman. "Model-Based Tool Assistance for Packet-Filter Design." *Proceedings of Workshop on Policies for Distributed Systems and Networks (POLICY'2001)*, January 2001.
14. A. Mayer, A. Wool and E. Ziskind. "Fang: A Firewall Analysis Engine." *Proceedings of 2000 IEEE Symposium on Security and Privacy*, May 2000.
15. R. Panko. *Corporate Computer and Network Security*, Prentice Hall, 2003.
16. J. Wack, K. Cutler and J. Pole. "Guidelines on Firewalls and Firewall Policy." *NIST Recommendations, SP 800-41*, January 2002.
17. T. Woo. "A Modular Approach to Packet Classification: Algorithms and Results." *Proceedings of IEEE INFOCOM'00*, March 2000.
18. A. Wool. "Architecting the Lumeta Firewall Analyzer." *Proceedings of 10th USENIX Security Symposium*, August 2001.

Chapter 2
Modeling and Verification of Firewall and IPSec Policies Using Binary Decision Diagrams

Abstract As firewall is the main front-end defense, IPSec is the standard for secure Internet communications, providing traffic integrity, confidentiality and authentication. Although IPSec supports a rich set of protection modes and operations, its policy configuration remains a complex and error-prone task. Unlike firewalls, IPSec exhibits more complex semantic that allows for triggering multiple rule actions of different security modes. This inherent complexity increases significantly the potential of policy misconfiguration and can violate the integrity of IPSec VPN security. Secure and safe deployment of IPSec requires thorough and automated analysis of the policy configuration consistency for firewall and IPSec devices across the entire network. In this chapter, we present a general composable model based on using Boolean expressions that can represent different ACL filtering semantics. We use this model to derive a canonical representation for firewall and IPSec policies using Ordered Binary Decision Diagrams. Based on this representation, we develop a comprehensive framework to classify and identify conflicts in a single firewall and IPSec device (intra-policy conflicts) or between different firewall and IPSec devices (inter-policy conflicts) in enterprise networks. Our testing and evaluation study on different network environments demonstrates the effectiveness and efficiency of our approach for identifying conflicts in firewall and IPSec policies.

2.1 Introduction

The Internet Protocol Security architecture (or IPSec) has been proposed by IETF to provide integrity, confidentiality and authentication of data communications over IP networks. The end users can specify the security level (AH or ESP) and mode (tunnel or transport) [12–14] to accommodate the traffic security requirements. IPSec devices typically encrypt and encapsulate the outgoing IP packets according to an IPSec *security policy*, while the receiving devices decapsulate and decrypt the incoming packets in order to verify integrity and authenticity. IPSec operations can be performed either at the traffic source and destination (transport mode) or at intermediate *security gateways* (tunnel mode) in order to allow for source-based or domain-based security respectively. Due to the flexibility and application transparency of IPSec, it is widely used today as a very cost-effective means to establish Virtual Private Networks (VPNs) or secure channels between corporate

© Springer International Publishing Switzerland 2014
E. Al-Shaer, *Automated Firewall Analytics: Design, Configuration and Optimization*, DOI 10.1007/978-3-319-10371-6_2

networks over the Internet. Using VPN, a user can establish secure IPSec sessions to security gateways in the protected network over the public or unprotected network. Users or administrators use the IPSec security policy to define IPSec protection operations for each specific traffic. The IPSec policy consists of lists of rules that designate the traffic to be protected, the type of protection, such as authentication or confidentiality, and the required protection parameters, such as the encryption algorithm [11]. Packets are sequentially matched against the rules until one (*single-trigger*) or more (*multiple-trigger*) matching rules are found [6, 12].

Deploying IPSec policy rules at many hosts and gateways provides incredible flexibility for customizing the appropriate protection mechanisms for different applications and network requirements. However, the lack of automated verification of IPSec security policies significantly increases the potential of policy inconsistency and conflicts allowing for more network vulnerability. Many challenges confront the verification of IPSec policy configuration in enterprise networks. First, the sequential rule matching and multi-trigger semantics make policy verification of single or distributed IPSec policies a very complex and error-prone task, particularly when large number of rules and devices exist. Second, the interaction between different IPSec policies, such as cascaded protection and overlapping tunnels, can lead to inefficient or incorrect data protection. Third, the existence of various action types (e.g., bypass, discard, encrypt/tunnel, authenticate/transport, etc.) poses another challenge when modeling and analyzing IPSec policies. Rule conflicts can occur due to IPSec misconfiguration within a single policy (called *intra-policy conflicts*) or due to the inconsistency between policies in different devices (called *inter-policy conflicts*). These conflicts may result in incorrect operation of IPSec and can lead to serious security threats including transmitting traffic insecurely, dropping legitimate traffic, and allowing undesired traffic into secure networks.

Therefore, successful deployment of IPSec security is highly dependent on the availability of policy management techniques that can analyze, verify and purify IPSec policy rules with minimal human intervention. Our contribution in this chapter comes in twofold. First, we present a generic model that uses Boolean expressions to capture the single-trigger and multi-trigger semantics of a wide range of filtering policies. Second, we introduce a novel framework that uses this model implemented in Ordered Binary Decision Diagrams (OBDDs) to provide comprehensive identification and classification of IPSec policy conflicts. Based on this framework, we developed a set of algorithms to discover intra- and inter-policy conflicts in any general IPSec policy configuration. We implemented these techniques in a tool called the "Security Policy Advisor" and showed that it is effective in discovering IPSec policy conflicts with acceptable processing and memory overhead.

Although IPSec has been deployed for many years, most of the related research work has been focused on addressing IPSec implementation problems. One related work [8] discovers the conflicts of overlapping IPSec tunnels using a simulation-based technique. Recent work [2] studies the policy conflicts particular to firewalls that are limited to "accept" and "deny" actions. Other related works [7, 10, 16] use a query-based approach to analyze firewall policies. None of the related work used formal methods to comprehensively identify IPSec policy conflicts. Therefore, we consider this work novel and significant not only in the area of IPSec but also for any filtering-based security policy such as firewalls and intrusion detection and prevention systems.

The rest of this chapter is organized as follows. In Sect. 2.2 we highlight the main components and present our formal model of the IPSec policy. In Sects. 2.3 and 2.4, we identify and define potential IPSec intra-policy and iter-policy conflicts respectively and we present techniques to discover them. In Sect. 2.5 we present a usability and performance study of our proposed techniques.

Finally, in Sect. 3.5 we present the summary of the chapter.

2.2 Modeling of Filtering Security Policies Using BDDs

In order to perform robust policy analysis, we need a solid and flexible model that is capable of capturing the underlying policy semantics. In this section, we show the components of IPSec policies, and present a formal model for any general filtering policy. We then apply this model to the IPSec policy components.

2.2.1 IPSec Policy Components

The protection offered by IPSec to certain traffic is based on requirements defined by security policy rules defined and maintained by the system administrator [6, 11]. In general, packets are selected for a packet protection mode based on network and transport layer header information matched against rules in the policy, i.e., transport protocol, source address and port number, and destination address and port number. To define traffic protection rules, the IPSec standard specifies the policy operational guidelines that should be implemented by vendors rather than a specific policy model [12]. In this work, we use a generic policy format that resembles the format used in a wide range of IPSec implementations [5]. This policy model is composed of two lists of packet-filtering rules:

2.2.1.1 Crypto-Access List

it consists of ordered filtering rules that specify actions to be performed on packets that match the rule conditions. All traffic is matched against the access rules sequentially until a matching rule is found. The matching rule action is either "protect" for secure transmission, "bypass" for insecure transmission, or "discard" to drop the traffic.

2.2.1.2 Crypto-Map List

the filtering rules in this list determine the cryptographic transformations required to protect the traffic selected for protection by the access list. A traffic may match multiple rules resulting in applying more than one transformation on the same traffic. Each rule is given a priority such that higher priority transformations are applied first.

$$access\_list := access\_rule[\ldots, access\_rule]$$

$$access\_rule := order, filter, action$$

$$filter := protocol, src\_ip, src\_port, dst\_ip, dst\_port$$

$$action := \text{protect} \mid \text{bypass} \mid \text{discard}$$

$$map\_list := map\_rule[\ldots, map\_rule]$$

$$map\_rule := priority, filter, transform\_list$$

$$transform\_list := transform[\ldots, transform]$$

$$transform := sec\_protocol, encaps\_mode, parameters$$

$$sec\_protocol := \text{AH} \mid \text{ESP}$$

$$encaps\_mode := \text{Transport} \mid \text{Tunnel } tunnel\_dst$$

Fig. 2.1 The syntax of IPSec policy statements

IPSec policy rules can be written using the syntax shown in Fig. 2.1. The *access_list* is used to define IPSec protection rules, while the *map_list* is used to define IPSec transformation rules. A *transform* is any cryptographic service that can be used to protect network traffic. These security services are IPSec AH and ESP protocols operating either in transport or tunnel mode along with the cryptographic algorithm and the necessary cryptographic parameters. Figure 2.2 shows an example of a typical outbound IPSec policy. The policy at each device is defined in terms of the access-list (upper section) and the map-list (lower section). In our work, we consider that inbound traffic arriving at a device interface is matched against a mirror image of the outbound IPSec policy of this interface, i.e., the inbound policy is similar to the outbound policy after swapping the packet filters for source and destination addresses [5].

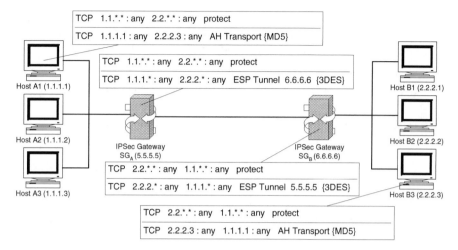

Fig. 2.2 Example of a typical IPSec configuration

2.2.2 Filtering Policy Representation

Although our discussion in this section will focus on IPSec filtering policies, the presented framework can be used to model and analyze generic filtering policies.

Definition 1. An *access policy*, $P = R_1, R_2, \ldots, R_n$, is a sequence of n filtering rules that determine the appropriate action performed on any incoming packet.

Definition 2. A *filtering rule*, R_i, consists of a set of constraints on a set of k filtering fields, $F = \{f_1, f_2, \ldots, f_k\}$, together with an action, a_i, from the set of all actions, A.

Each rule can be written in the form:

$$R_i := C_i \rightsquigarrow a_i$$

where C_i is the constraint on the filtering fields that must be satisfied for the action $a_i \in A$ to be triggered. The condition C_i can be represented as a Boolean expression over the filtering field values $fv_1, fv_2, \ldots, fv_k$ as follows:

$$C_i = fv_1 \wedge fv_2 \wedge \cdots \wedge fv_k$$

For IPSec, a filtering field value fv is typically given as a binary expression representing the binary value of a specific IP address (123.45.201.5), a block of IP addresses (123.45.201.*), a specific port number (80 for http) or a range of port numbers (137–139 for netbios). Finally, the actions allowed are simply protect, bypass or discard.

Definition 3. A *single-trigger access policy* is an access policy where only one action is triggered for a given packet. A *multi-trigger access policy* is an access policy where multiple different actions may be triggered for the same packet.

IPSec crypto-access rules form a single-trigger access policy. Once a traffic matches a certain rule, its action is triggered and no further matching is performed. This is in contrast to crypto-map rules where a particular traffic may match multiple rules causing multiple actions to be triggered.

2.2.2.1 Formalization of Single-Trigger Policies (Firewalls)

The semantics of a single-trigger policy $P = R_1, R_2, \ldots, R_n$ can be represented as a collection of Boolean expressions, $[[P]] = \{P_{act_1}, P_{act_2}, \ldots, P_{act_m}\}$, one for each possible action $act_m \in A$. The expression for an action should evaluate to true for all packets that trigger the action and false otherwise. The fact that $[[P]]$ is a single-trigger policy implies that, for any given packet, only one policy expression evaluates to true, and all other expressions evaluate to false. In general, we can construct a Boolean expression for P_a by using the rule constraints from each rule as follows:

$$P_a = \bigvee_{i \in index(a)} (\neg C_1 \wedge \neg C_2 \wedge \ldots \wedge \neg C_{i-1} \wedge C_i)$$

where $index(a)$ is the set of indices of rules that have a as their action. In other words,

$$index(a) = \{i \mid R_i = C_i \rightsquigarrow a\}.$$

This formula can be understood as saying that a packet will trigger action a if it satisfies the condition C_i for some rule R_i with action a, provided that the packet does not match the condition of any prior rule in the policy.

We express the IPSec crypto-access policy, S, as a single-trigger policy composed of a set of action expressions, *i.e.*, $[[S]] = \{S_{protect}, S_{bypass}, S_{discard}\}$. Therefore, based on the above formalization, the IPSec protection access policy $S_{protect}$ can then be defined as follows:

$$S_{protect} = \bigvee_{i \in index(protect)} (\neg C_1 \wedge \neg C_2 \wedge \ldots \wedge \neg C_{i-1} \wedge C_i)$$

2.2.2.2 Formalization of Multi-trigger Policies (IPSec)

The semantics of a multi-trigger policy $[[P]]$ can also be represented as a collection of Boolean expressions, one for each action allowed by the policy. Like the single-action case, the expression for an action should evaluate to true for all packets which trigger the action and false otherwise. Since $[[P]]$ is a multi-trigger policy, more than one action expression may evaluate to true for any given packet. Using the rule constraints from each rule, the Boolean expression for action $a \in A$ is constructed as follows:

$$P_a = \bigvee_{i \in index(a)} C_i$$

The formula means that a packet will trigger action a if it satisfies the condition C_i for any rule R_i with action a.

We express the IPSec crypto-map policy, T, as a set of expressions each of which represents the condition that triggers a specific transform, i.e., $[[T]] = \{T_{trans_1}, T_{trans_2}, \ldots, T_{trans_m}\}$ where T_{trans_m} could be for example $T_{\text{ESP-tunnel}}$, $T_{\text{AH-transport}}$ and so on. Thus, in general, the traffic transformation policy T_t that triggers a certain transform t can be represented as follows:

$$T_t = \bigvee_{i \in index(t)} C_i$$

2.2.2.3 Policy Representation Using OBDDs

The main objective of our policy representation as Boolean expressions is to formalize and facilitate policy analysis and rule conflict identification. The use of Boolean expressions allows us to use OBDDs [3] in our tool. OBDDs provide a canonical and concise representation for Boolean expressions and support all the common Boolean operations. Their usefulness can be highlighted by pointing out that two policies which are syntactically different (they have different rules) but are semantically equivalent (they exhibit identical behavior) will have the same OBDD representation. Policies can then be built up, combined, and compared using Boolean operations on the OBDDs representing them.

2.3 IPSec Intra-policy Analysis

In this section, we use our formal model to identify all possible types of conflicts that may exist in the policy of a single IPSec device. These conflicts may exist between rules in the crypto-access or crypto-map lists. We also prove that our conflict analysis is comprehensive.

2.3.1   *Classification and Discovery of Access-List Conflicts*

Access-list is a common component used in both firewall and IPSec devices. The ordering of access rules is crucial in determining firewall and IPSec access policy semantics. This is because the packet filtering process is performed by sequentially matching the packet against filtering rules until a match is found. If filtering rules are disjoint, the ordering of the rules is insignificant. However, it is very common to have filtering rules that are inter-related, i.e., exactly matched, inclusively matched or correlated [1]. In this case, if the related rules are not carefully ordered, some rules may never triggered because of other rules, resulting in an incorrect policy.

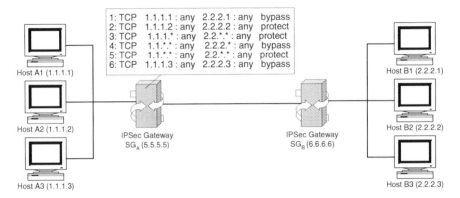

Fig. 2.3 Example for IPSec intra-policy crypto-access list conflicts

In this section, we classify different conflicts that may exist among the rules in an access policy and then describe a technique for discovering these conflicts.

We apply our policy model on IPSec crypto-access lists as a special case of the single-trigger policy. The policy expression S_a represents a policy that incorporates rule R_i, while S'_a represents the policy with R_i excluded.

2.3.1.1   Intra-policy Shadowing

A rule is shadowed when every packets that could match this rule is matched by some preceding rule with a different action. Subsequently, the shadowed rule will never be activated. Based on our OBDD representation, a rule is shadowed if the policy expression for the rule action does not change when this rule is removed, and the rule is not implied in the modified policy expression. Formally, rule R_i is shadowed if the following condition is *true*:

$$(S'_a = S_a) \text{ and } (C_i \rightarrow S'_a \neq true) \text{ and } (a_i = a) \quad (1)$$

The first condition means that the policy semantics does not change after removing the rule, while the second condition means that the rule condition is not included in the policy semantics.[1] As an example for this case, rule 6 is shadowed by rule 5 in Fig. 2.3. Shadowing is a critical conflict because the shadowed rule never takes effect. This might cause a desired traffic to be discarded or an undesired traffic to be bypassed.

2.3.1.2 Intra-policy Redundancy

A rule is redundant when every packets that could match this rule is matched by some other rule that have a similar action, such that if the redundant rule is removed, the security policy will not be affected. In OBDD representation, a rule is redundant if the policy expression for the rule action does not change when this rule is removed, and the rule is implied in the modified policy expression. Formally, rule R_i is redundant if the following condition is *true*:

$$(S'_a = S_a) \text{ and } (C_i \rightarrow S'_a = true) \text{ and } (a_i = a) \quad (2)$$

Referring to Fig. 2.3, rule 2 is redundant to rule 3. Redundancy is considered a conflict because a redundant rule adds to the size of the filtering rule list, increasing the search time and space requirements of the packet filtering process.

2.3.1.3 Intra-policy Correlation

A rule is in correlation with another rule if they have different filtering actions, and the preceding rule matches some packets that match the following rule and vice versa. Using OBDDs, a rule is in correlation with another rule if the policy changes when this rule is removed, and this rule is not fully implied in the policy expression. Formally, correlation exists if the following condition is *true*:

$$(S'_a \neq S_a) \text{ and } (C_i \rightarrow \neg S'_a \neq true) \text{ and } (a_i = a) \quad (3)$$

Rule 3 is in correlation with Rule 4 in Fig. 2.3. The two rules with this ordering imply that all traffic that is coming from 1.1.1.* and going to 2.2.2.* is protected. However, if their order is reversed, the same traffic will be bypassed. Correlation is considered a conflict because the relative order of the correlated rules affects the policy semantics.

---

[1] If the result of a OBDD operation does not evaluate to *true*, then it is either *false* or a *predicate* representing the resulting expression.

2.3.1.4   Intra-policy Exception

A rule is an exception of a following rule if they have different actions, and the following rule is a superset match. Based on OBDDs, a rule is an exception of a general rule if the policy changes when this rule is removed, and the rule is implied in the complement of the policy expression. Formally, exception exists if the following condition is *true*:

$$(S'_a \neq S_a) \text{ and } (C_i \rightarrow \neg S'_a = true) \text{ and } (a_i = a) \qquad (4)$$

Rule 1 is an exception of rule 3 in Fig. 2.3. These two rules imply that all the traffic coming from the address 1.1.1.* will be protected, except the traffic coming from 1.1.1.1. Exception is considered a non-critical conflict because sometimes it is desired to make an exception of a general rule. However, it is important to identify rule exceptions because they partially change the policy semantics and can lead to violation of the policy requirements.

Theorem 1. *The intra-policy access-list conflict conditions (Cases 1–4) are complete in the sense that every rule in a policy must satisfy one of the conflict conditions.*

2.3.1.5   Proof Sketch

The logical disjunction of the four conditions is equivalent to *true*. The complete proof can be found in [9].

Algorithm 1 discovers intra-policy access-list conflicts. The analysis is performed for every possible action in the access policy; i.e., protect, bypass and discard. The function BuildPolicyBDD(p, a) is used to derive the BDD of the policy expression that resembles the condition for policy p taking action a. The function BuildRuleBDD(r) constructs the BDD for the filtering condition of rule r. For every rule in the access list that has the same action, we build the policy BDD (S) as well

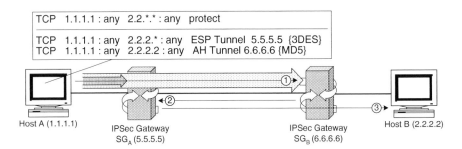

Fig. 2.4 Example for IPSec intra-policy overlapping-session conflicts

---

Algorithm 1 Intra-policy access-list conflict discovery

1: **for all** *action* in {protect, bypass, discard} **do**
2:    $S \leftarrow$ BuildPolicyBDD(*access_list*, *action*)
3:    **for all** *rule* in *access_list*
      and *rule.action* = *action* **do**
4:       $C \leftarrow$ BuildRuleBDD(*rule*)
5:       *test_list* $\leftarrow$ *access_list*
6:       RemoveRule(*test_list*, *rule*)
7:       $S' \leftarrow$ BuildPolicyBDD(*test_list*, *action*)
8:       *conflict* $\leftarrow$ NOCONFLICT
9:       **if** $S' = S$ **then**
10:         *test* $\leftarrow (C \rightarrow S')$
11:         **if** *test* = true **then**
12:            *conflict* $\leftarrow$ REDUNDANCY
13:         **else** {*test* $\neq$ true}
14:            *conflict* $\leftarrow$ SHADOWING
15:         **end if**
16:      **else** {$S' \neq S$}
17:         *test* $\leftarrow (C \rightarrow \neg S')$
18:         **if** *test* = true **then**
19:            *conflict* $\leftarrow$ EXCEPTION
20:         **else** {*test* $\neq$ true)}
21:            *conflict* $\leftarrow$ CORRELATION
22:         **end if**
23:      **end if**
24:      **for all** *test_rule* in *test_list* **do**
25:         *relation* $\leftarrow$ GetRuleRelation(*rule*, *test_rule*)
26:         **if** *conflict* $\neq$ NOCONFLICT
         and *relation* $\neq$ DISTINCT **then**
27:            **print** *conflict* between *rule* and *test_rule*
28:            **break**
29:         **end if**
30:      **end for**
31:   **end for**
32: **end for**

---

as the test BDD (S') (lines 2, 4–6). If both BDDs are identical, the rule is either redundant or shadowed based on testing if the rule is implied in S' (lines 8–14). If the BDDs are not identical and the rule implication test is true, then the rule is an exception of a more general rule, otherwise it is correlated to another rule in the policy (lines 15–22). To find the related rule, we sequentially match every rule in the policy against this rule and the first matching rule is reported (lines 23–29). The function GetRuleRelation($r1, r2$) gets the relation between rules $r1$ and $r2$ based on the definitions described in [1].

2.3.2   Classification and Discovery of Map-List Conflicts

Map-list is used uniquely by IPSec polices. In this section, we identify the rule conflicts that may exist in a single IPSec crypto-map list and result in security policy violation or unnecessary traffic protection.

2.3.2.1   Intra-policy Overlapping-Session Conflicts

IPSec allows nesting multiple IPSec sessions of different remote peers on the same traffic. In this case, in order to construct correct nesting, the traffic must be delivered to the closer peer first and then to the farther peer. In other words, in the map-list, the rule priority of the farther peer should be higher than the rule priority of the closer peer. This is mandatory because if the traffic is decapsulated at the farther peer first, it will be transmitted to the closer peer in the opposite direction, resulting in transmitting the traffic back to the destination without protection. The example in Fig. 2.4 illustrates this situation. In this example, two map rules apply to the traffic flowing from A to B. The first rule encapsulates the traffic in a tunnel to SG_A, then the second rule re-encapsulates the traffic in another tunnel to SG_B. The traffic is first received and decapsulated by SG_B and then forwarded back to SG_A. SG_A decapsulates the traffic and forwards it to B as clear text. Notice that this conflict can only occur with two tunneled transforms or with a transport transform followed by a tunnel. Other rule combinations will send the traffic to the same destination node. Also notice that if the nested sessions terminate at the same end point, the rule ordering is not required because all decapsulation will be performed at the same node.

Formally, the intra-policy overlapping-session conflict occurs when the following condition is *true* for any two tunnel-mode map-list rules R_i and R_j:

$$(C_i \wedge C_j \neq false) \text{ and } (i < j) \text{ and}$$
$$\text{Location}(R_i[tunnel\_dst]) < \text{Location}(R_j[tunnel\_dst]) \quad (5)$$

The first condition expresses the fact that the two rules must match some common traffic, and the other conditions verify that the tunnel end-point of the preceding rule comes before the tunnel end-point of the following rule in the path from $R_i[src\_ip]$ to $R_i[dst\_ip]$. A similar condition holds for any transport rule followed by a tunnel rule, but using $R_i[dst\_ip]$ instead of $R_i[tunnel\_dst]$. Later in Sect. 2.4.2.1, we prove that these conditions are comprehensive.

To discover intra-policy overlapping-session conflicts, we search for the rules that match the same traffic and satisfy the conflict conditions. The topology of the network can be encoded using OBDDs in a manner similar to what is done in symbolic model checking [4]. The location of every node can be encoded using OBDDs such that the locations of any two nodes can be retrieved and compared relative to a certain node. We start the analysis by finding every two rules that partially or completely overlap, thus matching the same traffic. A path conflict is reported if one rule specifies a tunnel transform terminating at a further point than the end point of a preceding overlapping rule. The full discovery algorithm and a detailed description of the technique are provided in [9].

2.3.2.2 Intra-policy Multi-transform Conflicts

IPSec also allows for multiple transforms to be applied to the same traffic simultaneously. This gives the user the flexibility to combine different IPSec protection methods to achieve the traffic security goals. However, some of these combinations provide weak protection, such as applying ESP transport after AH transport because ESP transport does not provide IP header protection. Moreover, other combinations may not improve traffic protection but cause performance overhead, such as applying AH tunnel followed by AH transport.

Formally, the intra-policy multi-transform conflict occurs when the following conditions are *true* for any two map-list rules R_i and R_j:

$$(C_i \wedge C_j \neq false) \text{ and } (i < j) \text{ and}$$
$$\text{Strength}(R_i[transform]) > \text{Strength}(R_j[transform])$$
$$\text{Location}(R_i[tunnel\_dst]) \geq \text{Location}(R_j[tunnel\_dst])(6)$$

Here we introduce the *transform strength* concept as the level of protection the transform provides for a particular traffic. For flexibility, the strength of any transform t_i can be user-defined, and we refer to it as Strength(t_i). If Strength(t_i)>Strength(t_j), then the transform t_i provides better protection than t_j, and vice versa. The first condition expresses the fact that the two rules must match some common traffic, and the second find if a weaker transform is applied on a stronger one. The third condition verifies that the tunnel end-point of the preceding rule comes after the tunnel end-point of the following rule in the path from $R_i[src\_ip]$ to $R_i[dst\_ip]$. A similar condition holds for any transport rule followed by a tunnel rule, but using $R_i[dst\_ip]$ instead of $R_i[tunnel\_dst]$. If the third condition is not true, the conflict reduces to the overlapping-session conflict described earlier in Sect. 2.3.2.1. We prove that these conditions are comprehensive later in Sect. 2.4.2.3.

Multi-transform intra-policy conflicts can be easily discovered by searching the map policy for rules that contain conflicting transforms. We start by building the OBDDs for map-list entries that include any two conflicting transforms. Then we get the intersection OBDD that represents the overlap condition where both transforms are applicable. For every map-list rule that intersects with the overlap condition, we check if it provides the weaker protection. In this case, a conflict is reported for this rule provided that the rule end point satisfies the location condition. The full discovery algorithm with detailed description are presented in [9].

2.4   IPSec Inter-policy Analysis

In this section, we identify all policy conflicts that may exist between any two different IPSec devices. These include conflicts between rules of the crypto-access lists or crypto-map lists in different IPSec devices. We also prove the comprehensiveness of our conflict analysis.

2.4.1   Classification and Discovery of Access-List Conflicts

Because of the decentralized nature inherent to the IPSec security policy, the potential of conflicts between policies in different IPSec devices is significantly high. Even if every IPSec device policy in the network does not contain any of the intra-policy conflicts described in Sect. 2.3, conflicts could exist between policies of different IPSec devices. For example, an upstream device might protect a traffic that is bypassed by a downstream device or vice versa. In the first case, the traffic will be dropped at the upstream peer because SA negotiation will fail. In the second case, the traffic will be dropped at the downstream peer because it will not be able to perform the decapsulation. In this section, we first define the conflicts that may exist between an upstream and a downstream access policy, and we then describe a technique to discover these conflicts. An example of such conflicts is shown in Fig. 2.5.

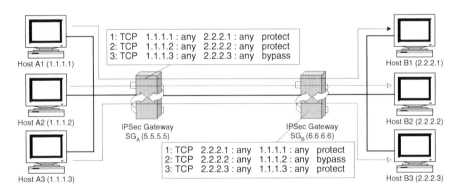

Fig. 2.5 Example for IPSec inter-policy crypto-access list conflicts

In this discussion, S^k resembles the access policy of an IPSec device D_k that exists along a certain network path. Also in our discussion, for simplicity and without loss of generality, we analyse the policies of only two devices on any network path, the upstream device (D_u) and the downstream device (D_d). However, the analysis can be performed iteratively on every two IPSec devices in the network in order to verify the IPSec policies in the entire network. Based on these assumptions, we can now formally define IPSec inter-policy conflicts as follows.

2.4.1.1 Inter-policy Shadowing

Traffic is shadowed if the upstream policy S^u blocks some traffic permitted by the downstream policy S^d. Formally, inter-policy shadowing exists if the following condition is *true*:

$$(S^{u}_{discard} \wedge \neg S^{d}_{discard}) \vee (S^{u}_{protect} \wedge \neg S^{d}_{protect}) \neq false \quad (7)$$

This expression represents the filtering condition that results in shadowing some traffic by D_u. The first term represents the traffic discarded by D_u but permitted by D_d while the second term represents the traffic that requires protection by D_u but is not protected by D_d. In this case, SA negotiation fails and the traffic is discarded at the upstream device. Rule 2 in SG_A and rule 2 in SG_B show an example of inter-policy shadowing. Shadowing is considered a conflict because it prevents the traffic desired by some nodes from flowing to the end destination.

2.4.1.2 Inter-policy Spuriousness

Traffic is spurious if the upstream policy S^u permits some traffic blocked by the downstream policy S^d. Formally, inter-policy spuriousness exists if the following condition is *true*:

$$(S^{u}_{bypass} \wedge \neg S^{d}_{bypass}) \vee (S^{u}_{protect} \wedge S^{d}_{discard}) \neq false \quad (8)$$

This expression represents the filtering condition that results in spurious traffic flowing to D_d. The first term represents the traffic permitted by D_u but not permitted by D_d, while the second term represents the traffic protected and permitted by D_u but discarded by D_d. Rule 3 in SG_A and rule 3 in SG_B show an example of inter-policy spuriousness. Spuriousness is a critical conflict because it allows unwanted traffic to flow into the network, increasing the network vulnerability to various network attacks such as port scanning, denial of service, etc.

Theorem 2. *The inter-policy access-list conflict conditions (Cases 7, 8) are complete in the sense that any policy inconsistency between two IPSec devices must satisfy one of the conflict conditions.*

2.4.1.3 Proof Sketch

For any packet, an upstream device may perform one of three actions: bypass, protect, or discard. For that same packet, a downstream device may perform one of the same three actions. These means there are nine possible combinations. The only combinations that do not satisfy one of the conflict conditions are combinations where the upstream device and the downstream device perform the same action. Clearly, these cases are not conflicts [9].

Algorithm 2 Inter-policy access-list conflict discovery

1: $S^u \leftarrow$ BuildPolicyBDD($D_u.access\_list$)
2: $S^d \leftarrow$ BuildPolicyBDD($D_d.access\_list$)
3: $C_{shadow} \leftarrow (S^u_{discard} \wedge \neg S^d_{discard})$
4: $C_{spurious} \leftarrow (S^u_{protect} \wedge S^d_{discard})$
5: **for all** $rule_u$ in $D_u.access\_list$ **do**
6:      $C_u \leftarrow$ BuildRuleBDD($rule_u$)
7:      $shadow\_test \leftarrow (C_{shadow} \wedge C_u)$
8:      $spurious\_test \leftarrow (C_{spurious} \wedge C_u)$
9:      **if** $shadow\_test \neq$ false **then**
10:         $conflict \leftarrow$ SHADOWING
11:     **else if** $spurious\_test \neq$ false **then**
12:         $conflict \leftarrow$ SPURIOUSNESS
13:     **else**
14:         $conflict \leftarrow$ NOCONFLICT
15:     **end if**
16:     **if** $conflict \neq$ NOCONFLICT **then**
17:         **for all** $rule_d$ in $D_d.access\_list$ **do**
18:             $C_d \leftarrow$ BuildRuleBDD($rule_d$)
19:             **if** $conflict =$ SHADOWING **then**
20:                 $test \leftarrow (C_{shadow} \wedge C_d)$
21:             **else if** $conflict =$ SPURIOUSNESS **then**
22:                 $test \leftarrow (C_{spurious} \wedge C_d)$
23:             **end if**
24:             $relation \leftarrow$ GetRuleRelation($rule_u, rule_d$)
25:             **if** $test \neq$ false and $relation \neq$ DISTINCT **then**
26:                 **print** $conflict$ between $rule_u$ and $rule_d$
27:                 **break**
28:             **end if**
29:         **end for**
30:     **end if**
31: **end for**

To discover these conflicts, we use Algorithm 2. Using the upstream outbound access policy and the downstream inbound access policy,[2] we construct the BDD for each of the conflict conditions defined above (lines 1–4). Each rule in the upstream policy is checked if it intersects with any of the conflict conditions (lines 6–15). If an intersection is found, we look for the corresponding rule in the downstream policy. Again, we match every rule in the downstream policy against the conflict condition until we find an intersecting rule (lines 16–23). If the downstream rule also matches the upstream rule, then the discovered conflict is reported along with the involved rules (lines 24–28).

---

[2]Recall that, in general, the inbound policy of an IPSec device is a mirror image of the outbound policy.

2.4.2   Classification and Discovery of Map-List Conflicts

In this section, we identify the conflicts that may occur between rules in different IPSec crypto-map lists and result in security policy violation or unnecessary traffic protection.

2.4.2.1   Inter-policy Overlapping-Session Conflicts

IPSec allows applying nested sessions on the same traffic at different points on the traffic path to multiple remote peers. Similar to the intra-policy case, the traffic must be transferred to the closer peer first and then to the farther peer. In other words, the packets should be decapsulated in reverse order of their encapsulation at subsequent points on the traffic path, otherwise unprotected traffic is transmitted to the destination. The example in Fig. 2.6 illustrates this case. In this example, two IPSec sessions are used to protect the traffic flowing from A to B. The sessions start at A and SG_A and encapsulate the traffic in tunnels terminating at SG_B and SG_C respectively. The traffic is first received and decapsulated by SG_C and then forwarded back to SG_B. SG_B decapsulates the traffic and forwards it to B as clear text. Notice that this conflict can occur with either two tunneled transforms, or a transport transform followed by a tunnel. Other rule combinations are not feasible because IPSec transport sessions cannot be initiated at intermediate security gateways.

Formally, the inter-policy overlapping-session conflict occurs when the following condition is *true* for any two tunnel-mode map-list rules R_i^u in the upstream device, and R_j^d in the downstream device:

$$R_i^u[src\_ip] \subseteq R_j^d[src\_ip] \text{ and}$$
$$R_i^u[tunnel\_dst] \subseteq R_j^d[dst\_ip] \text{ and}$$
$$\text{Location}(R_i^u[tunnel\_dst]) < \text{Location}(R_j^d[tunnel\_dst]) (9)$$

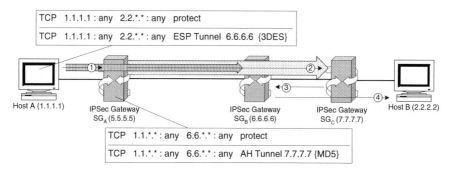

Fig. 2.6 Example for IPSec inter-policy overlapping-session conflicts

The first two conditions express the fact that the traffic that matches the upstream rule also matches the downstream rule. The last condition verifies that the tunnel end-point of the upstream rule comes before the tunnel end-point of the upstream rule in the path from $R_i^u[src\_ip]$ to $R_i^u[dst\_ip]$. A similar condition holds for any transport rule followed by a tunnel rule, but using $R_i^u[dst\_ip]$ instead of $R_i^u[tunnel\_dst]$ in the above condition.

Theorem 3. *The overlapping-session map-list conflict conditions (Cases 5, 9) are complete in the sense that any security violation must satisfy one of the conflict conditions.*

2.4.2.2 Proof Sketch

Nested IPSec sessions can start/terminate at the same node or at different subsequent nodes on the traffic path. Therefore, to create two nested IPSec sessions, we have six possible scenarios. Only two of these scenarios correspond to the decapsulation being performed in the wrong order. The conflict conditions are the formal descriptions of exactly these two cases [9].

A procedure similar to the one presented in Sect. 2.3.2.1 can be used to discover overlapping-session conflicts. For every upstream device D_u and downstream device D_d, we analyze the map-list rules that match the same traffic in both devices but terminate at different end points. Every outbound map-list rule in D_u is checked against all the inbound map-list rules of D_d. In tunnel mode rules, the source and destination filters are replaced by the tunnel end-points to resemble the resulting packet header. If any two rules overlap, and the downstream rule specifies a tunnel terminating at a farther point than the end-point of the upstream rule, a session conflict is reported. The full discovery algorithm and a detailed description of the technique are provided in [9].

2.4.2.3 Inter-policy Multi-transform Conflicts

IPSec also allows intermediate nodes to apply traffic protection on already protected traffic. However, this might be unnecessary and can cause extra overhead particularly if the new protection is weaker than the existing one. For example, applying an AH tunnel on traffic already encapsulated in an ESP tunnel does not improve the security protection. Formally, the inter-policy overlapping-session conflict occurs when the following condition is *true* for any two tunnel-mode map-list rules R_i^u in the upstream device, and R_j^d in the downstream device:

$$R_i^u[src\_ip] \subseteq R_j^d[src\_ip] \text{ and}$$
$$R_i^u[tunnel\_dst] \subseteq R_j^d[dst\_ip] \text{ and}$$
$$\text{Strength}(R_i^u[transform]) > \text{Strength}(R_j^d[transform])$$
$$\text{Location}(R_i^u[tunnel\_dst]) \geq \text{Location}(R_j^d[tunnel\_dst]) (10)$$

Similarly, the same condition holds for any transport rule followed by a tunnel rule, but using $R_i^u[dst\_ip]$ instead of $R_i^u[tunnel\_dst]$ in the above condition.

Theorem 4. *The multi-transform map-list conflict conditions (Cases 6, 10) are complete in the sense that any unnecessary protection between a pair of map-list rules must satisfy one of the conflict conditions.*

Proof Sketch

The two rules could be from the same policy or from different policies. If a pair of rules do not satisfy either of the conditions, then one or more of the following are true:

- There are no packets that match both rules.
- The protection offered by the earlier transform is weaker than the protection offered by the later transform.
- The second transformation is undone at a further point on the traffic path than the first transformation.

In the first two cases, the second transformation does provide some added protection. The third case is clearly an overlapping-session conflict.

Similar to the approach presented in Sect. 2.3.2.2, to discover this conflict we build the OBDDs for map list entries that include two conflicting transforms in two different IPSec devices. Then we get the intersection OBDD that represents the traffic condition where both transforms are applicable. For every rule in the downstream map-list, we verify that it does not provide the weaker protection when the location condition is satisfied. The full discovery algorithm with detailed description are presented in [9].

2.5   Usability and Performance Evaluation

We implemented the techniques and algorithms described in Sects. 2.3 and 2.4 in a software tool called the "Security Policy Advisor" or SPA. The tool implements the intra-policy and inter-policy conflict discovery algorithms presented in this chapter. The SPA was developed using the Java programming language and BuDDy, an OBDD package implemented in Java [15]. In this section, we focus our evaluation on the usability and the performance of the IPSec policy analysis techniques described in this chapter.

To assess the practical value of our techniques, we first used the SPA tool to analyze real IPSec policy rules in our university network as well as in some local industrial networks in the area. In many cases, the SPA has shown to be effective by discovering many policy conflicts that were not discovered by human visual inspection. We made an attempt to quantitatively evaluate the practical usability

Table 2.1 The percentage of administrators who created intra- and inter-policy conflicts in a manually written IPSec policy configuration

Experience	Access-list (%)	Overlapping-session (%)	Multi-transform (%)
	Intra-policy conflicts		
Expert (7)	14	14	0
Intermediate (12)	42	33	8
Beginner (19)	84	63	16
Conflict type (%)	19	9	7
	Inter-policy conflicts		
Expert (7)	29	14	14
Intermediate (12)	50	33	17
Beginner (19)	90	53	16
Conflict type (%)	38	16	11

of the SPA by conducting a set of experiments that consider the level of network administrator expertise. In this experiment, we created two IPSec policy exercises and recruited 38 network administrators with varying level of expertise in the field (7 experts, 12 intermediates and 19 beginners) to complete each exercise. The exercise included writing IPSec access list and map list rules based on a set of access-control policy requirements for 9 interconnected networks with 12 IPSec security gateways (intermediate and end-point gateways). We then used the SPA tool to analyze the rules and count different types of conflicts. The experiment results in Table 2.1 show the percentage of persons who introduced various types of conflicts in their IPSec policy configuration.

These results show clearly that even the expert administrators created policy conflicts. A total of about 29 % of experts created intra-policy and inter-policy conflicts. This figure is even much higher for intermediate and beginner administrators (a total of about 67 % and 90 % created intra-policy conflicts, and 75 % and 95 % created inter-policy conflicts respectively). An interesting observation is that most of the persons made mistakes in configuring access-list and overlapping-session rules. The table also shows the average ratio of each conflict type relative to the total number of discovered inter- and intra-policy conflicts. The results clearly indicate that access-list conflicts dominate the misconfiguration errors made by administrators (19 % intra-policy and 38 % inter-policy access-list conflicts).

In the second phase of our evaluation study, we conducted a number of experiments to measure the performance and the scalability of policy conflict discovery under different filtering policies and network sizes. Our experiments were performed on a Pentium PIII 600 MHz processor with 512 MB RAM (Fig. 2.7).

To study the performance of the intra-policy conflict discovery algorithms, we produced three sets of policy rules. The first set includes rules that have IP source and destination address ranges to resemble the best case scenario because OBDDs generated for these policies are small in size and faster in processing. In the second set, each rule has fully specified IP addresses for the source and destination, representing the worst case scenario because the corresponding OBDDs are large in size and require more processing and memory. The third set includes rules that are randomly selected from the two previous sets in order to represent the average case scenario and resembles a realistic IPSec policy. We used the SPA tool to run the intra-policy analysis algorithm on each set using various sizes of rule sets (10–100 rules). In each case, we measured the processing time and memory space needed to produce the policy analysis report. The processing time results we obtained are shown in Fig. 2.8a. Set 1 shows the least processing time, Set 3 is expected to have the highest processing, and Set 2 shows a moderate processing time. Even in the worst case scenario (Set 3), the processing time looks very reasonable; approximately 20–220 ms for 10–100 rules respectively. The memory space needed in the analysis is plotted in Fig. 2.8b. In the worst case, only 56 kB are needed to create the OBDDs used to analyze a policy of 100 rules.

For evaluating the performance of the inter-policy conflict discovery algorithm, we conducted a similar experiment on a network of IPSec devices resembling a realistic IPSec configuration. The topology is composed of several local networks connected globally to the Internet. Each network contains one IPSec security gateway and 30 IPSec enabled hosts protected by the gateway. Each host can establish IPSec sessions with 60 % of the hosts in other networks. We created three instances of the topology each with an different number of interconnected networks: three networks, six networks, and nine networks. For each IPSec node, we installed

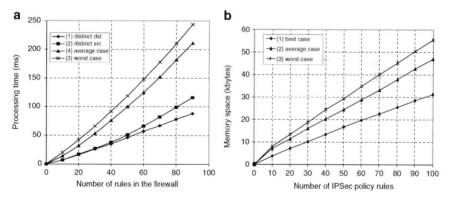

Fig. 2.7 Computational complexity of the intra-policy conflict discovery: (**a**) processing time; (**b**) memory space

a random set of IPSec rules to protect the traffic flowing to other networks. We then used the SPA to run the inter-policy analysis algorithms on every pair of interacting IPSec nodes in each topology with a varying number of policy rules (10–100 rules). For each topology, we measured the total processing time and memory space required to perform policy analysis. The processing time results are shown in Fig. 1.8a. We noticed that when the analysis is performed on a small number of networks, the processing time ranges from 40 s to 2 min. However, as more networks are involved in the analysis, the policy conflict discovery requires much higher processing time ranging from 1 to 18 min depending on the rule complexity. Figure 2.8b shows the memory space used in the analysis. The plot also reflects very reasonable memory requirements even for the large network (less than 3 MB). The quadratic increase in the processing time as the network size increases is due to the fact that the complexity of our techniques is dependant on the number of IPSec device pairs in the network. On the other hand, the memory used is linearly proportional to the number of devices because only one OBDD is built for each device, and a constant number of OBDDs is used to analyze pairs of IPSec devices.

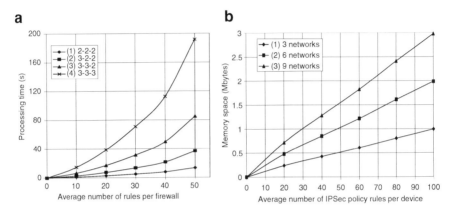

Fig. 2.8 Computational complexity of the Inter-policy conflict discovery: (**a**) processing time; (**b**) memory space

2.6 Summary

Although the IPSec standard provides various flexible data protection schemes for IP networks, configuring IPSec policies manually can be extremely complex and error-prone, particularly in enterprise networks. Hundreds to thousands of IPSec policy rules may exist in various devices. An exhaustive analysis of policy rules in all IPSec gateways is required to discover intra- and inter-policy conflicts and avoid serious network security threats like insecure transmission and flooding attacks. IPSec security, like any other technology, requires proper management support, including automatic conflict analysis and verification, in order to provide the required security services.

In this chapter, we attempt to bridge this gap by presenting (1) a new formal model that covers the semantics of a wide range of filtering policies including IPSec, and (2) a sound and complete framework for analyzing IPSec policy conflicts. The verification framework utilizes OBDDs, a well-known powerful verification tool that is widely used in many fields, to represent IPSec policies and derive solid formulation of policy conflicts. Based on this framework, we developed techniques for identifying rule conflicts in IPSec policies of a single device or across multiple inter-connected devices. Our approach is sufficiently general to be used for verifying many other filtering-based security policies such as firewalls, intrusion detection systems and access control devices. We show that our implementation of these techniques in a tool called the "Security Policy Advisor" is very effective in checking real-life IPSec policies. For example, our tool was able to discover conflicts in IPSec policies that were overlooked by up to 30 % of expert network administrators in our experiment. Our experiments have also shown that the average processing time in intra- and inter-policy conflict discovery is very reasonable for off-line analysis in many network configurations. For example, our Java implementation of the conflict discovery algorithms requires less than 4 min and 2 MB to analyze the entire IPSec policies for a considerably large network (180 IPSec devices with average 60 rules per device).

References

1. E. Al-Shaer and H. Hamed. "Modeling and Management of Firewall Policies." *IEEE eTransactions on Network and Service Management*, Volume 1-1, April 2004. http://www.etnsm.org/
2. E. Al-Shaer and H. Hamed. "Discovery of Policy Anomalies in Distributed Firewalls." *Proc. of IEEE INFOCOM'2004*, March 2004.
3. R. Bryant. "Graph-Based Algorithms for Boolean Function Manipulation." *IEEE Transactions on Computers*, August 1986.
4. J. Burch, E. Clarke, K. McMillan, D. Dill and J. Hwang. "Symbolic Model Checking: 10^{20} States and Beyond." *Journal of Information and Computation*, Volume 98-2, 1992.
5. "Configuring IPSec Network Security." *Cisco IOS Security Configuration Guide, Release 12.2*, Cisco Systems, Inc.
6. N. Doraswamy and D. Harkins. *"IPSec: The New Security Standard for the Internet, Intranets, and Virtual Private Networks"*, second edition. Prentice Hall PTR, March 2003.
7. P. Eronen and J. Zitting. "An Expert System for Analyzing Firewall Rules." *Proc. of 6th Nordic Workshop on Secure Systems*, November 2001.
8. Z. Fu, F. Wu, H. Huang, K. Loh, F. Gong, I. Baldine and C. Xu. "IPSec/VPN Security Policy: Correctness, Conflict Detection and Resolution." *Proc. of Policy'2001 Workshop*, January 2001.
9. H. Hamed, E. Al-Shaer and W. Marrero. "Design and Implementation of Security Policy Advisor Tools." *Technical Report: CTI-TR-05-010*, May 2005. http://www.mnlab.cs.depaul.edu/projects/SPA/files/spa-tr05010.pdf
10. S. Hazelhurst, A. Attar and R. Sinnappan. "Algorithms for Improving the Dependability of Firewall and Filter Rule Lists." *Proc. of IEEE Workshop on Dependability of IP Applications, Platforms and Networks*, June 2000.
11. K. Jason, L. Rafalow and E. Vyncke. "IPsec Configuration Policy Information Model." *RFC 3585*, IETF, August 2003.
12. S. Kent and R. Atkinson. "Security Architecture for the Internet Protocol." *RFC-2401*, IETF, November 1998.
13. S. Kent and R. Atkinson. "IP Authentication Header (AH)." *RFC 2402*, IETF, November 1998.
14. S. Kent and R. Atkinson. "IP Encapsulating Security Payload (ESP)." *RFC 2406*, IETF, November 1998.

15. J. Lind-Nielsen. "The BuDDy OBDD package." http://www.bdd-portal.org/buddy.html
16. A. Mayer, A. Wool and E. Ziskind. "Fang: A Firewall Analysis Engine." *Proc. of IEEE Symposium on Security and Privacy (SSP'00)*, May 2000.

Chapter 3
Specification and Refinement of a Conflict-Free Distributed Firewall Configuration Language

Abstract Multiple firewalls typically cooperate to provide security properties for a network, despite the fact that these firewalls are often spatially distributed and configured in isolation. Without a global view of the network configuration, such a system is ripe for misconfiguration, causing conflicts and major security vulnerabilities. We propose *FLIP*, a high-level *firewall configuration policy language* for traffic access control, to enforce security and ensure seamless configuration management. In FLIP, firewall security policies are defined as high-level service-oriented goals, which can be translated automatically into access control rules to be distributed to appropriate enforcement devices. FLIP guarantees that the rules generated will be conflict-free, both on individual firewall and between firewalls. We prove that the translation algorithm is both sound and complete. FLIP supports policy inheritance and customization features that enable defining a global firewall policy for large-scale enterprise network quickly and accurately. Through a case study, we argue that firewall policy management for large-scale networks is efficient and accurate using FLIP.

3.1 Introduction

A firewall is a collection of component, interposed between two networks, that filters traffic between them according to some security policy. The security policy is defined based on the broad and diverse security requirements of user communities and implemented as sequential filtering rules in firewall. Single firewall relies on network topology restriction to enforce the policies and perform the filtering. The filtering decision is taken according to the order of the filtering rules. The firewall always takes the action of the first matching rules for each packet. But, a firewall policy may include intra-firewall anomalies, where a packet may match with two or more different filtering rules. When the filtering rules are defined, serious attention has to be given to rule relations and interactions in order to determine the proper rule ordering and guarantee correct security policy semantics. As the number of filtering rules increases, the difficulty of add a new rule or modifying an existing one also increases.

To make things even worse, due to the increasing of line speed and the more computational intensive protocol, firewall tend to become congestion points in

© Springer International Publishing Switzerland 2014
E. Al-Shaer, *Automated Firewall Analytics: Design, Configuration and Optimization*, DOI 10.1007/978-3-319-10371-6_3

current large scale network. Furthermore, the assumption that every one on the protected network is trusted for single firewall model may not hold anymore. To avoid the performance bottleneck and security vulnerability induced by the centralized firewall approach, additional internal firewalls have to be deployed. In distributed firewall system, the security policies are defined centrally but enforced distributively at each enforcement point (firewall) [11]. Thus, firewalls might also have inter-firewall anomalies when individual firewalls in the same path perform different filtering actions on the same traffic. Therefore, the administrator must give special attention not only to all rule relations in the same firewall in order to determine the correct rule order, but also to all relations between rules in different firewalls in order to determine the proper rule placement in the proper firewall.

As the size and complexity of current large-scale network has increased, traditional manual and isolated configuration of firewalls has been proved inadequate to bridge the gap between the high-level security requirement and low-level device implementations. However, the security requirement to a large-scale network can only be enforced correctly when all the distributed firewalls cooperate together. Managing the security policy in such a large and heterogeneous environment is a difficult task: the final security policy is the combination of the local policy of each firewalls. How can one resolve these conflicts to produce non-conflicting local policies that satisfy the desired global security requirements? Further, how might one verify that the security device configurations are complied with the security requirement?

Although a lot of research works have been done about firewall security, the emphasis was mostly on the filtering performance issues [5, 7, 14]. Only few related work [3, 6, 10] attempt to address the conflict problems in high level policy and then map to filtering rules. But none of the previous works give a significant attention to address anomalies detection, rule translation and distribution in distributed firewalls environment. The importance and complexity of enforcing security and ensuring seamless firewalls configuration convince us that a complete security policy management framework is needed in current large-scale network. So, in this chapter, we will propose a distributed architecture to address the automatic firewall policy management problem in enterprise network, in which the cumbersome tasks including policy definition, rule distribution and enforcement, and conflicts resolution are automated. The whole policy design and enforcement process will be as follows: First, the user uses this language to define the firewall policy in an abstract level like there is only one firewall in the network through policy designator. Then the user compiles the language to find the conflicts and resolve them. Then based on the network topology and firewall distribution, the policy translator translate the high level policy to low level rules and the policy distributor will distribute the policy to each firewall. The main objectives of this architecture are as follows:

- The security policy should be clearly defined without ambiguity and anomaly free. In FLIP, the security policy is defined as high-level service-oriented goals with FLIP language, rather than device related configuration rules, that can then be translated into rules distributed in firewalls automatically.

- All conflicts in security policy should be detected and resolved. With the language grammar restriction and runtime checking by FLIP policy designator, the final policy will be conflict free.
- Automatically distribute firewall policy with respect to the network topology without introducing inter-firewall anomaly, and reconfigure at each firewall in response to the change in global and local firewall policy. In this approach, we decouple the security policy and network topology during the policy definition. The user can define the high level security policy without the knowledge of network topology. The policy distributor will distribute each rule to the according firewall to ensure the security semantics.

The rest of this chapter is organized as follows. In Sect. 3.2, we describe the system architecture, syntax and semantics of FLIP language, as well as the the design principles that guided us to the system. We introduce the algorithms for policy translation and distribution. We prove that the translation exactly preserves the high-level semantics of FLIP, and the distribution is anomaly free. We present a case study in Sect. 3.3, demonstrating the utility of the language. We discuss the scalability and performance of rule translation Sect. 3.4. In Sect. 3.5, we present the summary of the chapter.

3.2 FLIP System Architecture

FLIP covers the whole network security policies management processes from policy definition, distribution to policy enforcement in each firewall, as shown in Fig. 3.1. This section describes the functionality of the main components in FLIP. First, we introduce the policy designator with focus on the FLIP policy language and conflict resolution. Later, we describe the policy translator and distributor, and prove why the algorithm used in FLIP can guarantee no anomaly exists in FLIP system.

3.2.1 Policy Designator

Policy designator provides the user interface of FLIP system, through which the user can submit the security policy, resolve the conflicts based on the runtime conflict detection results. The first step to automatic distributed firewall policy management is to provide a high level policy language. The policy defined with this language should reflect the security requirement of the administrator no matter what mechanisms used to implement the policy. The policy in FLIP can also be defined with the equivalent XML file.

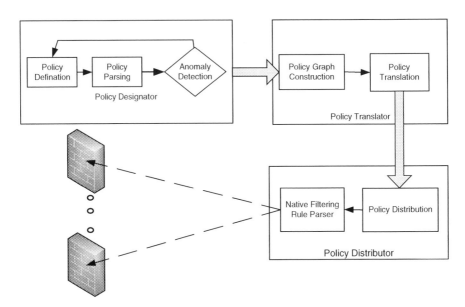

Fig. 3.1 FLIP system architecture

3.2.1.1 FLIP Language Specifications

We propose FLIP language with following desired features, which make it suitable for defining and managing security policies in a large-scale network:

- Service-oriented: The language should focus the user's attention on the security requirements of network services rather than low-level traffic details as in the rule-oriented approach.
- Modular and reusable: The language objects are self contained and can be reused and extended to scale to large networks.
- Rule order independent: The user should be able to define the security policy in any order without worrying about introducing conflicts.
- Conflict free: The compiled policies should not have conflicts in a single device (intra-policy) or across multiple devices (inter-policy).

In this section we present in detail each of the basic constructs comprising FLIP and show the above principles are embodied in the syntax and semantics of FLIP.

3.2.1.2 Key Language Constructs and Grammar

FLIP includes constructs to describe *services*, *rules*, *policy groups* and *domains*. Rules define the action performed on the traffic flow of specific network service that satisfy the rule conditions. A policy group is a logical unit which aggregate related rules together and can be applied on domains. The grammars and relationships of these constructs are detailed below.

```
<domain_def> ::= "domain" <domain_name> "=["
                 <domain> { "," <domain> }
                 "]"
    <domain> ::= <ip_address> ["/"<submask> ] | <ip_range>
                 | <domain_name> { <operator> <domain> }
   <service> ::= <protocol> ".["
                 <predicates>
                 "]" { "," <service> }
  <protocol> ::= "tcp" | "udp" | "icmp" | "ip"
<predicates> ::= <predicate> { ("," | "OR") <predicate> }
 <predicate> ::= <field_name> <operator> <value>
```

Fig. 3.2 Domain and service definition syntax

Domain. A domain is a logical unit which contains the network addresses of entities (workstations, servers and network devices) that share the same security requirements. The entities in one domain can come from different physical subnets. A domain can be defined by a set of IP ranges, IP addresses with wildcard or host names. Also, one domain can be constructed by combining other domains. A domain can be viewed as a special set contains only network address, so we can apply the set operations on domain: intersection ($*$), union ($+$), subtraction ($-$). The syntax of domain definitions is shown in Fig. 3.2, in EBNF. As usual square braces indicate optional items and curly braces indicate potentially empty repetition. The following example defines a domain *students*:

Service. A service is defined as the combination of a protocol name and a set of properties associated with that protocol. Each property of a protocol is a predicate which is defined by the field name in that protocol header, the operator and value of that field. The field names in common protocol headers have been predefined in FLIP and the supporting protocols can be extended if needed in the future. Predicates can be linked together using the logical operator *AND* and *OR*, where the comma represents *AND*. The syntax of service definition is shown in Fig. 3.2.

For example, tcp.[dst_port = 80] means http traffic. One service can represent multiple traffic flows in the network as long as those traffic flows can satisfy the conditions defined in the properties set. For example, tcp.[dst_port > 2045, dst_port < 3078] represents all tcp traffics with destination port between 2045 and 3078. We can define the yahoo instant messaging (*yahoo_msg*) and Bit Torrent [4] (*torrent*) service as follow:

Policy Group. A policy group is a aggregation and abstraction of detail rules which are related to a set of entities (domains, hosts). A policy group consists of a set of service blocks. Each service block consists of rules associated with that specific network service. The rules in each service block are not complete firewall rules which contains all the five tuples (source address, source port, destination address, destination port, and protocol). For incoming traffics, the destination addresses are undefined, and for outgoing traffics, the source addresses are undefined. So in FLIP, a policy group should be applied on a policy target (domains, hosts) to complete

```
<group> ::= "policy_group" <name> [ "extends" <name> ] "{"
            [ "incoming:" <block> ]
            [ "outgoing:" <block> ]
            "}"
<block> ::= [ "enforce" | "restrict" ]
            ( <service_name> | <service> ) "{"
            { <rule> }
            "}"
 <rule> ::= [ "enforce" | "restrict" ]
            ( "allow" | "deny" )
            <domain> { "except" <domain> } ["to" <domain> ]
```

Fig. 3.3 Policy group definition syntax

the rules. The policy targets shared the same policy group can receive or send out the same types of traffic. In each policy group, the incoming and outgoing services are organized int two service groups. The syntax of policy group definition is shown in Fig. 3.3. The following example shows the definition of a simple policy group which block the yahoo instant messaging and Bit Torrent downloading but allow access to the internet.

Apply Policy Group on Domains. In FLIP, we allow multiple policy groups to be applied to a single domain. The syntax of applying policy groups on domains is shown in Fig. 3.4. We can apply the policy group student_policy on domain students as follow:

```
apply student_policy on students
```

```
<apply_block>          ::= "apply" <policy_set> "on"
                           <domain_set>[<dynamic_resolution>]
 <policy_set>          ::= <policy_group_name>
                           { "," <policy_group_name> }
 <domain_set>          ::= <domain_name>
                           { ("+"|"-"|"*"|",") <domain_name> }
<dynamic_resolution> ::= "{" <res_rule>  {"," <res_rule>}"}"
<res_rule>             ::= <service_id><rel_operator><service_id>
<service_id>          ::=<policy_group_name>"."<service_name>
```

Fig. 3.4 The syntax of applying policy groups on domains

Policy Group Hierarchy and Inheritance. In order to increase the modularity and reusability of the policy group, we organize policy groups hierarchically. Every policy group specifies its parent group, similar to the superclass specification in common object-oriented languages. If no parent group is specified, the default virtual policy group is assigned as the parent group. FLIP only allows single inheritance: each policy group can extends from only one parent group. This restriction enforces a tree structure on policy groups, making inheritance relationships between policy group clear and helping users locate sources of conflict.

Restrict and Enforce Rules. There are two special types of rules in FLIP: *restrict* and *enforce*. Restrict rules are visible only in the current policy group and can not be inherited by child groups. Restrict rules are used to define special policy which should only be applied to special domain. Restrict rules can also be used to define policies for those services in which parent and child have different policy. Enforce rules can not be overwritten by child policy group, which are used to define those policies the administrator want to be enforced across multiple domains without any violation. Enforce rules must be inherited by child group.

3.2.1.3   Conflict Detection and Resolution

An extensive study [2, 9] shows that various conflicts can happen between rules in single or distribute firewalls. One of the most important objectives of FLIP is to help user design and enforce security policies without introducing conflicts. The policies defined by FLIP should exactly reflect the security requirements without any ambiguity. FLIP handles the conflicts from the following three perspectives.

Static Conflict Resolution

Static conflicts are those conflicts introduced during policy groups definition which can exist between rules in single policy group or parent and child policy groups.

Conflict in Single Policy Group. In order to prevent conflict existence in policy group, FLIP has two constraints for policy group:

- The rules in each service block must be disjoint. This means that there should be no overlapping between the source or destination address between different rules for the same service.
- The services in incoming or outgoing traffic block must be totally disjoint. For example, `tcp.[dst_port = 80]` service can not coexist in the same incoming traffic block with service `tcp.[dst_port < 1024]`.

The first restriction guarantees no conflicts between rules in the same service block; the second, between services in same direction. These two constraints ensure that no conflicts can occur between rules in same policy group.

Conflicts Between Parent and Child Policy Group. Conflicts can be introduced when parent and child group have different rules for same services. Whereas the high level rules defined in the FLIP language are order-independent, the low-level rules generated during translating are order-sensitive. FLIP resolves the conflicts between parent and child policy group by adjusting the order of low level rules for child group generated by FLIP rule translation algorithm. Conflicts between parent and child are resolved assuming that the child group specifies a more detailed security policy which further reflect the user's objective. So FLIP gives the rules in child group higher priority than the rules in parent group, unless they conflict with the `enforce` rules of the parent: these rules may not be overridden by child policies. The high priority of rules in child group and enforced rules in parent group is reflected by the rules order in the generated low level rules. The translation is explained in Sect. 3.2.2.3.

The following example shows the conflicts in single policy group and between parent and child policy group. We now define a new policy group `dom_std_policy` which contains the security policy for students live in university dormitory. The security objectives are the following: (1) allow students use yahoo instant messaging, (2) block the online game *World of Warcraft* [15] (tcp, dst_port=3724), (3) block web proxy cache squid (tcp, port 3128) because it can also be used by Trojans and (4) allow windows remote desktop (tcp, port=3389) from network 140.192.*. In order to block both *World of Warcraft* and *squid*, the administrator in dormitory choose the block all tcp traffic use port between 3100 and 3800. The policy is shown below:

We can easily see that there is a conflict between blocking all tcp service using port from 3100 to 3800 and allow windows remote desktop. Also, there is another conflict between parent and child group for service *yahoo_msg*.

Dynamic Conflict Resolution

Dynamic conflicts are those conflicts introduced when applying policy groups on domains. Different association between policy groups and domains may create different conflicts.

Conflicts Between Policy Groups Applied on Same Domain. Different policy groups may have different policies for same service. Conflicts can be introduced when one domain (or subdomain) is applied with more than one policy groups. This situation can happen under one of the following two scenarios:

- If two or more policy groups must be enforced in a single domain, those policy groups are explicitly applied on that domain.
- When two or more domains share some common network addresses and each domain is applied with different policy group, the common part is implicitly applied to more than one groups.

For the first scenario, FLIP resolves the conflicts between policy groups based on the sequence in which these policy groups are applied on the domain. The earlier policy groups applied first are given higher priority. For example, `apply p1, p2 on D` specifies that both policy group `P1` and `P2` should be applied on domain `D`, and that `P1` should be given higher priority. If conflicts exist, the rules in high priority policy group overwrite the rules in low priority policy group. The conflicts can be detected at compilation time, and indeed our compiler gives the error reports about the conflicts for the common addresses. This allows the user to resolve the conflicts by explicitly applying the policy groups with correct order.

Conflicts Between Policy Groups Applied on Different Domain. When multiple policy groups applied on different domains, conflicts may occur for inter-domain traffics. Please see below for a simple example. If we define and apply policy group like this, there will be a conflict for the ssh traffic between domain D_1, and D_2. The ssh traffic from D_1 to D_2 will be allowed to leave domain D_1 but will be denied to access D_2.

There are two types of conflict resolution techniques can be used to resolve this type of conflict: prevention and rule delegation.

In prevention approach, no rules will be allowed in the outgoing block of each policy group if the destination is an internal domain. Only rules defined in the incoming block of each traffic group control inter-domain traffic. The violation of this constraint will be detected at run time by the FLIP compiler. The internal domains are those domains whose IP range are covered by the organization's IP addresses and whose traffic can be controlled by organization's firewalls. For previous example, since D_1 and D_2 are internal domain, the rule in P_1's outgoing block of allow ssh traffic to D_2 can not exist and FLIP compiler will suggest user to remove it.

But there is a disadvantage with prevention approach. It introduces unnecessary traffic (the ssh traffic sent from D_1 will be blocked by D_2) in the network. So in FLIP, we adopt the rule delegation approach. In this approach, after applying policy groups on domains, if the destination domain want to block a internal traffic from another domain, this rule will be delegated by adding an enforced deny rule for that traffic in the policy group which is applied on the source domain. In previous example, the deny rule for ssh traffic in P_2 will be delegated by adding enforce deny rules in P_1. After compilation, policy group P_1 is defined like follow:

But be advised that only the P1 instance which is applied on D1 is changed by rule delegation. The P1 instances applied on other domain will not be changed.

Fine Grained Dynamic Conflict Resolution. Resolve conflicts only based on the sequence of policy group for a domain may not be enough in some situation. For example, if we apply policy group P_1 and P_2 on domain D_1. For http service, we want the rules in P_1 has high priority, but for ftp service, we need rules in P_2 overwrite rules in P_1. In order to provide fine grained dynamic conflict resolution, we introduce the dynamic resolution block when apply multiple policy groups. The previous example can be resolved as follow: The rules defined in dynamic resolution block will overwrite the priority implied by the sequence of the policy groups for specified service.

3.2.1.4 FLIP Expressiveness

With the wide acceptance and installation of Cisco router, the access control list (ACL). In Cisco IOS can be viewed as the de facto standard for packet filtering. So we study the expressiveness of FLIP language by comparing FLIP with ACL. An ACL is a sequential collection of permit and deny conditions that apply to IP addresses. The Cisco IOS software tests addresses against the conditions in an access list one by one. The first match determines whether the software accepts or rejects the address. If no conditions match, the software rejects the address. Extended access lists use both source and destination addresses for filtering and allow filtering by protocol type, The language format is shown below:

Lemma 1. *Any IP packet filtering rule defined in ACL can also be written in FLIP.*

Proof. We prove this lemma by showing that every field in ACL is also supported in FLIP. Both the ACL and FLIP support same action types (permit and deny). The equivalency between of definition of IP address and wildcard in these two language is obvious. Both languages support filtering packets based on protocol. In ACL, the port number can be defined with optional operator. Possible operands include lt (less than), gt (greater than), eq (equal), neq (not equal), and range (inclusive range) which requires two port values. The operands lt, gt, eq, neq and neq with port in ACL can be defined in FLIP with single predicate $port < | > | = |! = portValue$. The inclusive port range can be defined with two predicates with format $port < value1, port > value2$ since the implicit "AND" relation between predicates in FLIP. The optional "established" in ACL indicates an established connection, which can be defined in FLIP with predicate $SYN = 1\ OR\ RST = 1$. The optional "fragments" in ACL targets noninitial fragments of packets, which can be defined in FLIP with predicate $IP.FragmentationOffset > 0$. Through this comparison, we can see that every field in ACL is supported in FLIP.

The expressiveness of ACL is also determined by the language semantics. Based on the relations between rules in ACL, we have the following lemma.

Lemma 2. *Suppose rule R_1 and R_2 are two rules in same ACL, any relations between rule R_1 and R_2 can also be written in FLIP.*

Proof. Without losing generality, we assume R_1 has lower rule order than R_2. The relation between R_1 and R_2 belongs to one of the following five distinct relations: completely disjoint, exact match, inclusive match, partially disjoint and correlated [1]. The union of these relations represents the universal set of relations between any two filtering rules in ACL [1]. We prove this lemma by showing that each of these five possible relations between R_1 and R_2 can be written in FLIP.

- Complete disjoint means every field in R_1 is not a subset and not a superset and not equal to the corresponding field in R_2. This relation has no impact on packets filtering, we don't need do anything in FLIP.
- Exact match means every field in R_1 is equal to the corresponding field in R_2. Then, R_2 is redundant, we only need define according rule for R_1 in FLIP.
- Inclusive match means every field in R_1 is a subset or equal to the corresponding field in R_2. We can remove R_1 without any impact on the filtering result. So, in FLIP we only need define according rule for R_2.
- Partially disjoint means there is at least one field in R_1 that is a subset or a superset or equal to the corresponding field in R_2, and there is at least one field in R_1 that is not a subset and not a superset and not equal to the corresponding field in R_2. If the protocols are not equal in these two rules or protocols are equal

but the ports in these two rules are disjoint, that means R_1 and R_2 are targeting different network traffic. So we don't need do anything special in FLIP, just define according rule for each of them. Otherwise, the rules can be defined in FLIP as follows:

If two rules have same action, we can combine two rules together in FLIP. Since domain in FLIP can be created by the union of subdomain. We can create the source domain and destination domain by the union of source and destination ip in R_1 and R_2. Then we create new service in FLIP by the protocol and the union of ports in R_1 and R_2.

If R_1 and R_2 have different action, we need take the following steps to define the rules: First, define disjoint services. Suppose $R_1.ports$ and $R_2.ports$ represent the set of ports defined in R_1 and R_2. If $R_1.ports = R_1.ports \cup R_2.ports$ or $R_2.ports = R_1.ports \cup R_2.ports$, that means the ports in one rule is a superset of ports in another rule. We can separate the ports into two disjoint sets: $R_1.ports \setminus R_2.ports$ and $R_2.ports \setminus R_1.ports$. Then define two services by combining protocol with each set of ports. If $R_1.ports \subset R_1.ports \cup R2.ports$ and $R_2.ports \subset R_1.ports \cup R2.ports$, then we can separate ports into three disjoint sets: $R_1.ports \setminus R_2.ports$, $R_2.ports \setminus R_1.ports$ and $R_1.ports \cap R_2.ports$. We can define then three disjoint services. Second, define disjoint source and destination domain. Suppose $R_1.src\_ip$ and $R_1.dst\_ip$ represent source and destination IP address in R_1. Then we can define two disjoint source domains: $R_1.src\_ip$ and $R_2.src\_ip \setminus R_1.src\_ip$ and two disjoint destination domain: $R_1.dst\_ip$ and $R_2.dst\_ip \setminus R_1.dst\_ip$. Third, define rules. In each service block, we can define two disjoint rules with disjoint source domains, the rule defined with source domain $R_1.src\_ip$ has $R_1.action$, the other rule with $R_2.action$. Fourth, apply defined policy to the two disjoint destination domains.

- Correlated means some fields in R_1 are subsets or equal to the corresponding fields in R_2, and the rest of the fields in R_1 are supersets of the corresponding fields in R_2. We can apply the same procedure as partially disjoint to define FLIP rules. Due to the space limit, the details are not repeated here.

We have enumerated all possible relations between R_1 and R_2, this complete the proof.

Based on previous two lemmas, we have the following theorem:

Theorem 3.1. *FLIP language has the same expressiveness as the ACL language.*

3.2.2 Policy Refinement and Translation

The policy defined with FLIP must be translated into lower level rules in order to be enforced by a firewall. Translation uses an intermediate language of common-format packet-filtering rules: high-level policies are translated into common format rules, and then the common format rules are translated to specific device configurations. It is crucial for that these steps not introduce ambiguous or false low-level rules.

Algorithm 3 policyTranslation

1: **if** exist conflicts **then**
2:      stop and send conflict reports
3: **else**
4:      PGRules()
5:      construct policy graph
6:      **for** each domain $d \in G$ **do**
7:          $d.status \leftarrow undistributed, d.parent \leftarrow NULL$
8:      **end for**
9:      $r.parent \leftarrow NULL, Q \leftarrow \emptyset$
10:     $ENQUEUE(Q,r)$
11:     **while** $Q \neq \emptyset$ **do**
12:         $d \leftarrow DEQUEUE(Q)$
13:         **for** each adjacent domain $da = ajcent(d)$ **do**
14:             **if** $da.status = undistributed$ **then**
15:                 $da.status \leftarrow predistribution$
16:                 $ENQUEUE(Q,da)$
17:             **end if**
18:         **end for**
19:         put rules from each policy group related to into $list_d$ based on the priority and dynamic resolution
20:         $distribute(list_d)$
21:         $d.status \leftarrow distribted$
22:     **end while**
23: **end if**

Algorithm 4 PGRules

1: **for** each policy group P **do**
2:      $P.state \leftarrow unfinish$
3: **end for**
4: **for** each P with $P.state = unfinish$ **do**
5:      $ruleGeneration(P)$
6: **end for**

In this section, we introduce our rule translation algorithm and show its sound-ness and completeness: that is, the output IL program exactly captures the semantics of the original FLIP program.

3.2.2.1 Semantics of the Intermediate Language

The common-format packet filtering rules (also called IL, or intermediate language) have the format: The source and destination IP addresses in IL rules may include wildcards and subnet masks.

A *packet* consists of a header and data. An IL program determines whether a given packet is accepted or denied by going through the rules in order. The first rule header that matches the packet header determines the outcome (accept or deny).

Algorithm 5 ruleGeneration. Input: policy group P

```
 1: if P.state = unfinish then
 2:     put enforced rules at the top of high-level policy definition
 3:     ER ← translate enforce rules of each service
 4:     NR ← translate normal rules of each service
 5:     Q ← P.parent
 6:     if Q = NULL then
 7:         P.Rules.add(ER)
 8:         P.Rules.add(NR)
 9:     else
10:         parentRules ← ruleGeneration(Q)
11:         P.Rules.add(parentRules.ER)
12:         P.Rules.add(ER)
13:         P.Rules.add(NR)
14:         P.Rules.add(parentRules.NR)
15:     end if
16:     P.state ← finish
17: end if
18: return P.Rules
```

The semantics of an IL program is given as a pair (A, D) where A is the set of packets accepted by the program and D is the set of packets denied by the program. Clearly A and D must be disjoint. Note that if no rule header matches a packet, then the packet is neither accepted or denied. Two IL programs are equivalent if the accept and deny exactly the same packets.

3.2.2.2 Semantics of FLIP

In the next subsection we present an algorithm that translates FLIP into IL. Let A_{FLIP} be the accept set of the original FLIP program and let A_{IL} be the accept set of the IL program which is the result of translation. The translation is *sound* if $A_{IL} \subseteq A_{FLIP}$ and *complete* if $A_{FLIP} \subseteq A_{IL}$, and similarly for the denied sets.

To give a compositional semantics for FLIP, we consider a slightly richer model than that used for IL. The meaning of a rule (or a group of rules such as a policy group applied to a domain) is a four-tuple (A, D, EA, ED), where each element of the tuple is a set of packets.

- A represents the packets accepted by the rule and D represents the packets that are denied by the rule. Packets that are neither explicitly accepted nor explicitly denied will not appear in either A or D.
- EA (resp. ED) stand for the packet-headers that correspond to the *enforced* allow (resp. deny rules).

The following invariants hold: $EA \subseteq A$, $ED \subseteq D$, $A \cap D = \emptyset$, and $EA \cap ED = \emptyset$. The four-tuples carry redundant information used for combining FLIP programs together. When finally executed, the sets A and D determine the packets accepted and denied.

Definition 1. A FLIP program with meaning (A, D, EA, ED) is *equivalent* to an IL program with meaning (A', D') if $A' = A$ and $D' = D$.

We understand the inheritance construct of FLIP denotationally as an operation on four-tuples. Let $P_1 = (A_1, D_1, EA_1, ED_1)$ and $P_2 = (A_2, D_2, EA_2, ED_2)$. Then $P' = (A', D', EA', ED')$ represents the result of P_1 extends P_2, where

$$ED' = ED_2 \cup [ED_1 \backslash EA_2]$$
$$EA' = EA_2 \cup [EA_1 \backslash ED_2]$$
$$D' = [D_1 \backslash EA_2] \cup [D_2 \backslash A_1] \cup [ED' \backslash EA']$$
$$A' = [A_1 \backslash ED_2] \cup [A_2 \backslash D_1] \cup [EA' \backslash ED']$$

The rest of the FLIP constructs are semantically straightforward. Thus, we can associate a semantics as a four-tuple (A, D, EA, ED) with every FLIP program.

3.2.2.3 Rule Translation Algorithm

FLIP performs conflict discovery before translation. The high-level policies are translated into low-level rules only when all conflicts have been resolved [1]. The rule translation in FLIP is based on network topology and the policy groups applied on each domain (logical). The relations between domains and between domain and policy groups can be represented with policy graph. The policy graph is constructed as follows: we use the one virtual node as root which stand for all internal network addresses. Based on the network topology, if all traffic of a domain can be covered by a single firewall, this domain is mapped to a node in the graph. Otherwise, one domain can be divided into a set of subdomains as each subdomain can be covered by a firewall. Due to conflict resolution, the common IP addresses shared by multiple domains will be removed from those domains to become a separate domain if the common part contains resolved conflicts. This domain will be mapped to a node in policy graph as well. If two domains have parent and child relationship, then we connect them with a solid line. Each node associates with a policy vector which contains all the policy groups applied to it. Please see Fig. 3.8 for a simple example of policy graph. In this graph, domain D5 and D6 are divided into two subdomains. FLIP translates and generates low level rules for each domain based on the policy graph. The high level node (domains) in the graph will be translated first. The rationale behind this is that the low level rules has rule order. The large domain need be translated first, thus the rules for subdomain will be on top of the result rule list.

The top-level rule generation algorithm is shown in Algorithm 3. After the rule translation for each policy group, FLIP ANALYZES the assignment between policy groups and domains to construct the policy graph. Then the policy translator performs a breadth first search for policy graph, translate the policy for each domain. We can see that after policy translation, the low level rules will be distributed for each domain. The rule distribution will be detailed in next section.

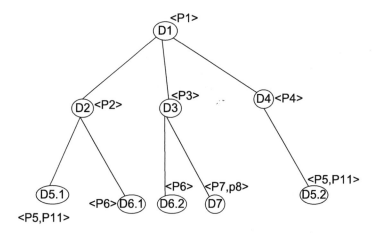

Fig. 3.5 Policy graph examples

Fig. 3.6 Format of low level
rules generated by algorithm

In order to translate high-level policy into low-level common format filtering rules, FLIP generates rules for each policy group, as described in Algorithm 4 (Fig. 3.5).

Each policy group is then translated into low-level rules, as described in Algorithm 5.

Because of the constraints imposed in Sect. 3.2.1.3, there can be no overlapping between high level rules in the same policy group. So, in each policy group, we can process each collection of high-level rules separately and modularly. The disjointness also permits us to construct convenient orderings of the low-level rules. In our representation, we always put the low-level rules corresponding to the enforced rules at the top (of each policy group)—see the diagram in Fig. 3.6.

The algorithm works modularly with respect to the constructs of FLIP. Figure 3.7 shows an example of how the low level rules from parent policy group are inherited by child policy group. On the sides of the picture, we have pictorial representations of the low-level rules that implement the enforce rules (ER) and normal rules (NR) of the parent and the child. The picture in the middle illustrates the result of inheritance. The resulting rule order is consistent with the hierarchical relation between policy groups—the enforce rules (ER) from parent group are put on top of the rule list, then the local enforce rules. After that, the normal rules (NR) from local policy group and normal rules form parent group are put into rule list sequentially.

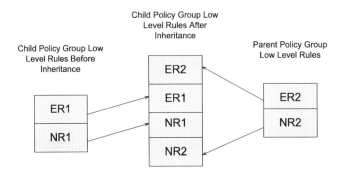

Fig. 3.7 Illustration of translation algorithm for inheritance

3.2.3   *Results*

We prove that our translation of the inheritance combinator of FLIP preserves equivalence.

Lemma 3. *Let the translation of policy group P_1 (resp. P_2) be equivalent to P_1 (resp. P_2). Then the policy group P_1 be extended from policy group P_2 is equivalent to its translation given by the algorithm.*

Proof. The proof is based on boolean algebra manipulations. We sketch the operational intuitions underlying the equivalence by tracing the accept/deny decisions.

When policy group P_1 extended from P_2 algorithm 5 adds enforced rules of P_2 to the top of low level rules list. Then it adds the enforce rules of P_1 into the rules list. The rule order guarantees that the enforce rules from parent group will be matched first. So the `enforce allow rules` of P_1 after translation will be the union of `enforce allows rules` with the `enforce allow rules` of P_1 from P_2 that are not already denied by the `enforce deny rules` of P_2, i.e.

$$T(EA_1') = EA_2 \cup [EA_1 \setminus ED_2].$$

Similarly, we can get the required equivalence for $T(ED_1')$.

Based on the rule order, the `normal allow rules` defined in P_1 will be hit if the combined enforce rule can not match the packet. And the `normal allow rules` defined in P_2 can only be hit if both the combined enforce rules and the normal rules defined in P_1 can not match the packet. So the total allow rules will be the union of the `enforce allow rules` $(EA_1' \setminus ED_1')$, `normal allow rules` in P_1 (A_1) that are not denied in P_2 (ED_2) and the `normal allow rules` in P_2 (A_2) that are not already denied in P_1 (D_1). So we get

$$T(A_1') = [A_1 \setminus ED_2] \cup [A_2 \setminus D_1] \cup [EA_1' \setminus ED_1'].$$

Similarly, we can get the required equivalence for $T(D_1')$.

Algorithm 6 Distritbute

1: **for** each service s of incoming traffic **do**
2:      $Q_r \leftarrow groupRule(s, d_s)$
3:      **for** each $IRL \in Q_r$ **do**
4:          deploy IRL to the most upper-stream firewalls in the traffic path
5:          remove all deny rules from IRL and deploy the rest rules to all the firewall along the traffic path
6:      **end for**
7: **end for**
8: deploy outgoing rule of d_s to the closest firewall

This is the key case of the proof since the priorities between multiple policy groups on a domain is also resolved in a fashion analogous to inheritance of policies. So, we have the desired theorem:

Theorem 3.2. *Any FLIP program is equivalent to the IL rules generated for that program by the translation algorithm.*

3.2.4 Policy Distributor

After rule translation and generation, the IL rules need to be distributed to firewalls to implement the high level policies. The distribution process must guarantee that no policy anomaly has been introduced. In a single firewall environment, the local firewall policy may include intra-firewall anomalies. Moreover, in distributed firewall environments, firewalls might also have inter-firewall anomalies. Therefore, the rule distribution algorithm must not only guarantee the correct rule order in single firewall, but also analyze all relations between rules in different firewalls in order to determine the proper rule placement in the proper firewall.

The basic idea of rule distribution algorithm is to keep the rule order of each service for each domain's incoming traffic intact and group related rule together into a indivisible rule list (IRL). Each IRL is a set of rules whose order must be maintained and must be allocated together into the same firewall. Each IRL will be deployed to the FLIP controlled firewall which is closest to the source. From previous section we already know that during rule generation, the rules related to same domain have been generated together, and the rules order keep the IL rules equivalent to high level FLIP policy. Thus, when we group related rules for each service, we only need search the rules for same domain. The rules for outgoing traffic will be deployed to the closest firewall. The algorithm of deploy rules for one domain is shown in Algorithm 6.

3.2.4.1   Policy Integrity

It is very important to maintain the policy equivalency after policy distribution. That means the rule distribution will not block any expected packets or accept any unexpected packets. The distributed firewalls should work together as same as a single firewall.

Theorem 3.3. *Rule distribution in FLIP can maintain the policy equivalency.*

Proof. From rule distribution algorithm, we can see that each rule can only be distributed along the firewall in its path. And the policy sequence is maintained by deploy rules based on the policy graph from root to leaf. Thus, the more detail rules of subdomain will be put on top of each firewalls. Without losing generality, suppose we have two policy domain $D_1 \in D_2$. Suppose D_1 is applied with policy P_1 and D_2 with P_2. If only single firewall f_2 exists for D_2, then the policy deployed on f_2 should be $R_{f_2} = R_1 \cup (R_2 \backslash R_1)$. If there are two firewalls f_2 for D_2 and f_1 for D_1, then after distribution, the rules for D_1 will be distributed to both f_1 and f_2 first, then the rules for D_2 will be distributed to f_2. Then the aggregated policy for d_1 will be $(R_1 \backslash R_2) \cap R_1 = R_1 \backslash R_2$.

This guarantees that no accept packets to subdomain will be blocked by more general rules of parent domain. Let R_f represent the rules deployed in firewall f, then we can get the following:

$$\bigcap_f R_f = R_{total}$$

Also, based on the distribution algorithms, we know that, rules are distributed along all the traffic path for each domain. So no unexpected packets be accepted.

3.2.4.2   Intra-firewall Anomalies

Lemma 4. *Rule distribution will not create intra-firewall anomalies in any firewall.*

Proof. In any given firewall, the rules are ordered based on the downstream domains or subdomains position in policy graph. The rules of leaf domains put on top of the rules of domains in higher level. Also, for each domain, the related rules for each service have been grouped into same IRL. The rule order of each IRL is as same as rules in IL translated by FLIP engine. In each firewall, each packet can only match rules in one rule set because the destination domain and service type. So, there will be no anomaly between rules in different IRL in single firewall. In each IRL, although the packet can match more than one rules, but the rule order guarantee the matching result consistent with the high level FLIP policy semantics. There is no ambiguity for low level rules in each firewall.

3.2.4.3   Inter-firewall Anomalies

Lemma 5. *Rule distribution will not create inter-firewall anomalies between firewalls.*

Proof. All inter-firewall anomalies have been studies in [1]. We use the same anomalies definition in our discussion. Because rules for each downstream domain or subdomain will be deployed first, and the IRLs of each service have been deployed to all the firewalls along the traffic path. So the traffic accept by downstream firwall can not be blocked by upstream firewalls. There is no shadowing anomaly.

For the same reason, the external traffic denied by downstream firewall can not be allowed by upstream firewall. And due to the rule delegation, the internal traffic denied by the destination domain will not be allowed to leave the source domain. So, there is no spurious anomaly.

The deny rules for each rule set are deployed to the most upstream firewall only, no downstream firewall will be deployed the same rule again. So there is no redundancy anomaly.

Finally, along the traffic path, each packet can only match rules in one IRL. There is no correlation between rules in different IRL from different firewall. Also, the rule order in same IRL has been proved to guarantee the high level filtering semantics. So there is no correlation anomaly. We have covered all possible inter-firewall anomalies. This complete the proof.

Based on Lemmas 4 and 5, we can have to following theorem.

Theorem 3.4. *Rule distribution in FLIP is anomalies free.*

3.3   A Case Study

Through the following example, we show how FLIP can be used to define and deploy security policies in a large-scale network environment. We use as a case study the network of an academic institution. The network is separated into two campus: Downtown and North Park. Each campus is composed by a set of departments, administration offices, research labs, servers (mail, FTP, Web, etc.), and the desktop of faculties and staffs. Based on the information sensitivity, research and administration activities, each department, office,lab or group of users may have different security requirements. We use a fraction of the security policies defined based on the security requirements to demonstrate the usability and expressiveness of FLIP. These policies by no means cover all the security requirements in real life deployments. The security requirements are outlined as follows (Fig. 3.8):

- Allow internal network users to access any Web server on the Internet by using HTTP or HTTPS except certain cites in blacklist which should be blocked.

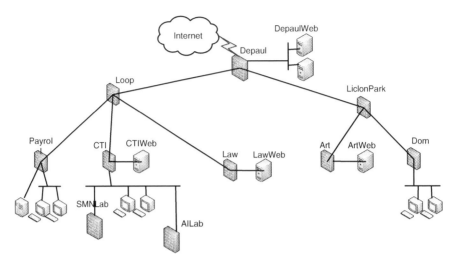

Fig. 3.8 The topology of an academic institution network

- Allow access to the internal Web server, DNS server located at Demilitarized zone (DMZ).
- Block internal users to access FTP servers on the internet except faculties and administrators machines, block FTP request from internet to any internal FTP server.
- Allow AOL and MSN instant messaging, but block MSN file transfer for students' computers in North Park Dormitory.
- Block windows terminal services from internet except faculties and research labs.
- Block windows terminal services, SSH [13], FTP, telnet request from any staffs' machine to important internal servers located at 140.192.60.1–140.192.60.15
- Allow administrators to use windows terminal service to access any window based machines.
- All labs must not allow SSH access from machine other than the network administrators' machine.
- It is recommended (but not enforced) to prevent students in labs to access Bittorrent search engine www.isohunt.com.
- If it does not violate the research lab general policy, smnlab would like to allow incoming multicast traffic and to allow student access any web page.
- For research purpose, the internet user must be able to access the FTP server (140.192.37.129) in smnlab. Also, the internet user must be able to access the peer-to-peer application running at machines (140.192.37.130–140.192.37.133) in smnlab.

The domains and services used in this example can be defined as follows: First we define the policy group Institution_Policy which is the general policy for the academic institution: We can define the policy for DMZ as follows:

Table 3.1 Average finishing time and number of anomalies of the policy definition experiment

Experience	Time man-written (min)	Time with FLIP (min)	Man-written conflicts	FLIP conflicts
Expert	30	17	7	0
Intermediate	51	24	13	0
Beginner	75	32	17	0

Then we extend `Institution_Policy` to define the policy for different departments, labs, faculties and stuffs. The general policies for research can be defined as follows: Now we can define the policy for multimedia networking lab (`mnlab`). Please be aware that the policy of http traffic to yahoo defined in `Lab_Policy` is overwritten by the policy defined in `mnlab_Policy`. Although, the policy in `mnlab_Policy` try to allow multicast traffic, it conflict with the enforce rule inherited from `Lab_Policy`. So multicast traffic can not reach `mnlab`. Through this example, we can see how the enforce rule is kept during policy group inheritance.

The policy for admin and faculty ca be defined by extending the general global policy group (Institution_Policy) as follow: After define all the policy and domain, now we can apply the policy groups on domains.

Because there is an intersection between `staff` and `admin` domain, the common part of these two domains will be applied with two policy groups. There is a conflict between policies for terminal service. For the common part we explicitly resolving the conflicts by giving `admin` high priority; thus the intersection between `admin` and `stuff` will be able to access terminal services.

From this case study we can see that FLIP is very suitable to design and implement security policies with FLIP in large scale distributed firewalls environment. In the tested network, we have two campus with multiple firewalls. The faculty, students and stuff are located in both campus. Their traffics are filtered by a set of firewalls. FLIP can easily handle this complicated topology because FLIP group the targets share with same security policy in one domain. Although the members can come from different subnets. Also, by modularity and inheritance, FLIP greatly reduce the policy need to be defined by the administrator. The policy translation and distribution module will take care of the tedious configuration of each device and guarantee the security integrity (Table 3.1).

3.4 Implementation and Evaluation

We implemented the techniques and algorithms described in this chapter in a software module called FLIP tool. The implemented tool, FLIP, performs conflict detection and low-level rule generation. The implementation is built in Java. In this section, we present our evaluation study of the usability and the performance of the FLIP.

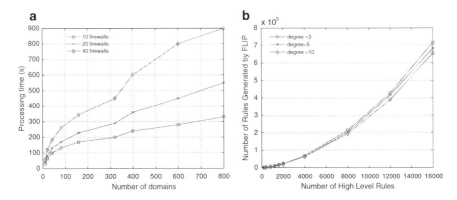

Fig. 3.9 FLIP Processing time, include conflict resolution, policy translation and distribution, and the generated rules number changes as degree. (**a**) FLIP processing time, include conflict resolution, policy translation and distribution. (**b**) The generated rules number changes as degree

3.4.1 FLIP Usability

To assess the practical value of our techniques, we used the FLIP to design some real firewall rules based on different security requirements. FLIP has shown to be effective by reducing the policy development time without introducing conflicts. We then attempted to quantitatively evaluate the practical usability of FLIP by conducting a experiments that consider the level of network administrator expertise, the developing time and number of anomalies in the final result. In this experiment, we created a firewall policy exercise and asked 12 network administrators with varying level of expertise in the field to complete the exercise. The network administrators are separated into two groups, each group has equal numbers of administrators in same level. The exercise is to write firewall rules based on a given security policy requirements. The total number of rules was around 60 in a network having only three firewalls. The results of this experiment are shown in Fig. 4.2. We can see that with the help of FLIP, the beginner can complete the experiment in almost half the time needed by the expert with no conflicts.

3.4.2 Scalability and Performance

In second part of our evaluation study, we conducted a number of experiments and simulation to measure the performance and the scalability of FLIP. We deploy FLIP on a network of an academic institution, which contains several campuses, departments and multiple firewalls. We start our experiments with small number of domains and involved firewalls, use FLIP to analyze the defined policy and distribute the low level rules to each firewall. We increase the number of target domains, the

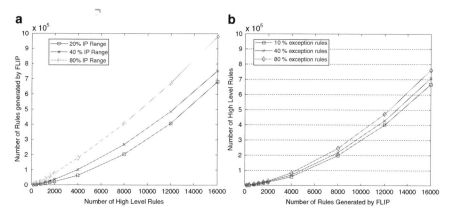

Fig. 3.10 The generated rules number changes as percent of domains defined by IP Range changes and as percent of exception rules change. (**a**) Percent of domains. (**b**) Perception of exception rules

related policy groups and firewalls to evaluate the performance of FLIP in large scale distributed networks with complicated policy. The FLIP engine was installed on a machine with Pentium PIII 1 GHz processor and 1 GB memory. The processing time needed as the change of domains and firewalls is shown in Fig. 3.9.

We then conducted some simulation to evaluate the scalability of FLIP. We produced three sets of policy groups and domains definition. In first set, there is no intersection between target domains on which the policy groups are applied. In second set, 20 % of target domains have overlapping, and in third set, 40 % of target domains have overlapping. Our simulation target a B class IP network, we assume each policy group explicitly defines 20 high level rules, and each policy group is applied to a different domain. We use FLIP to analyze these policy groups to find conflicts with various number of policy groups. The result shows clearly that as the percentage of intersecting domains increase, the time needed to detect the conflicts increase. This is because each domain intersection is applied with more than one policy group, the rules from different policy groups need to be analyzed together to detect the conflicts.

3.4.3 The Number of Rules Generated by FLIP

The number of rules generated by FLIP is crucial to the firewall performance, since running time to find a match increases linearly in the number of rules [8]. Our goal is to avoid generating unnecessary or redundant rules. FLIP translate the rules into general firewall configuration format, like the format in IPTables [12]. That means the source and destination can not be defined as IP Range. So the domain defined by IP Range have to be break in to sub-domain which can be defined with network address and subnet masks. Due to the policy group inheritance and domain (IP range) separation, the number of low level rules generated by FLIP is larger than the explicitly defined rules in high level policy groups. In the example in Sect. 3.3, we define eight domains, six network services and six policy groups, after translation, FLIP generates 48 low level rules.

In this section, we evaluate the rules generated by FLIP under different scenario and try to identify the key factors which influence the rule numbers. There are three factors which contribute to the number of rules generated by FLIP engine: policy group inheritance, domain definition, and number of exception rules. We evaluate their influence separately. For this study, we continue use the previous setting (each group has 20 high level rules).

The Impact of Policy Group Inheritance. We control the inheritance relationships between groups by define the maximal child group each parent can possible has (degree). The smaller the degree, the larger the depth of the tree. This means child groups inherit more rules from parent groups. In this experiment, we assume there are 20 % domains defined by IP range, and 20 % of high level rules have exception. We generate a set of policy groups and a set of domains. We fix the relation between the policy group and domain, conduct the experiment with different degree values. The result of number of low level rules is shown in Fig. 3.10. For this result, we can see that the change of degree does not influence the final rules number much.

The Impact of Domain Definition With IP Range. In this study, we fix the degree $= 5$, exception rules ratio equal 20 %. We control how many percentage of domain are defined with IP Range, and study its impact on the rule generation. The result is shown in Fig. 3.10a. From this figure, we can see that as the percentage of domains defined with IP Range increase, the rules number increase evidently. This is because the more the domains defined with Ip Range, the high the possibility that these domains have overlapping. More overlapping domains may introduce more conflicts. Since our approach breaks large overlapping domains into small disjoint subdomains to resolve the conflicts for each subdomains, as the overlapping domains increase, the number of rules generated by FLIP also increases.

The Impact of Exception Rules. Exception rules need be translated specially in our approach, it need more than one rules to represent the user's objectives. We fix the degree equal to 5, 20 % of domains defined with IP range, and study the number of rules changes as the percentage of exception rules change. The result is shown in Fig. 3.10b. From this figure, we can see that with exception rules increase, the total low level rules does not increase much.

3.5 Summary

Managing security policy in large-scale enterprise network requires a fixable policy definition, conflicts resolution and rule distribution. Simply having firewalls on the network boundaries or between sub-domains may not necessarily make a network any more secure. Misconfiguration of security devices due to rule conflicts or policy inconsistency may increase network vulnerabilities. In this chapter, we proposed a new high-level firewall policy language (FLIP) to manage distributed firewalls globally and transparently. FLIP is a service-oriented language that focuses on the service security requirements, unlike rule-oriented languages that impose traffic detail in the configuration. FLIP allows network administrators to define their high-level security goals that are then translated to rules and distributed in the firewall devices automatically. The generated rules are order-independent and conflict-free for intra- or inter-firewall configuration. The FLIP modularity and reusability exhibited by the policy group definition greatly reduce the time and effort to define firewall policies and generate rules in a large-scale enterprise networks. The hierarchical structure of policy groups improves the understanding of the interaction between the global and local policies. We also show the soundness and completeness of our rule translation algorithm. So, FLIP can guarantee the consistency between the security policy definition groups and the enforcement points.

In our evaluation study, we have shown that using FLIP enables the network administrators with little experience to design the firewall policies faster and more accurately than experts in the field. In regards to performance, although the policy group analysis are parabolically dependant on the number of policy groups and the number of rules in each group, our experiments show that the average processing time for conflicts discovery is very reasonable for practical applications. Using our Java implementation of the FLIP engine, our results indicate that, in case of 80 % of domains are intersected with each other, it takes 56–1103 ms of processing time to analyze 10–90 (200–1800 rules) policies groups. We also show that the number of rules generated rules by FLIP is very comparable to the rules defined manually in IPTables format.

References

1. Ehab Al-Shaer and Hazem Hamed, Discovery of Policy Anomalies in Distributed Firewalls,In Proceedings of IEEE INFOCOM'04, March 2004
2. Ehab Al-Shaer and Hazem Hamed, Taxonomy of Conflicts in Network Security Policies, IEEE Communications Magazine, Vol. 44, No. 3, March 2006
3. Y. Bartal., A. Mayer, K. Nissim and A. Wool. Firmato: A Novel Firewall Management Toolkit. *Proceedings of 1999 IEEE Symposium on Security and Privacy*, May 1999.
4. BitTorrent http://www.bittorrent.com/
5. Z. Fu, F. Wu, H. Huang, K. Loh, F. Gong, I. Baldine and C. Xu. "IPSec/VPN Security Policy: Correctness, Conflict Detection and Resolution." *Proceedings of Policy' 2001 Workshop*, January 2001.
6. J. Guttman. "Filtering Posture: Local Enforcement for Global Policies." *Proceedings of 1997 IEEE Symposium on security and Privacy*, May 1997.
7. B. Hari, S. Suri and G. Parulkar. "Detecting and Resolving Packet Filter Conflicts." *Proceedings of IEEE INFOCOM'00*, March 2000.
8. Hazem Hamed and Ehab Al-Shaer, Dynamic Rule-ordering Optimization for High-speed Firewall Filtering, *ACM Symposium on InformAtion, Computer and Communications Security (ASIACCS'06)*, March 2006.

9. Hazem Hamed, Ehab Al-Shaer and Will Marrero, Modeling and Verification of IPSec and VPN Security Policies. *In Proceedings of IEEE ICNP'2005,* November 2005.
10. S. Hinrichs. "Policy-Based Management: Bridging the Gap." *Proceedings of 15th Annual Computer Security Applications Conference (ACSAC'99),* December 1999.
11. S. Ioannidis, A. Keromytis, S. Bellovin, and J. Smith. Implementing Distributed Firewall. *Proceedings of Computer and Communications Security (CCS), pages 190"C199,* November 2000.
12. IPtables http://www.netfilter.org/
13. Tatu Yl "onen SSH — secure login connections of the internet. *In Proceedings of the Sixth USENIX Security Symposium, San Jose, California, USA,* July 1996.
14. T. Woo. "A Modular Approach to Packet Classification: Algorithms and Results." *Proceedings of IEEE INFOCOM'00,* March 2000.
15. World of Warcraft http://www.worldofwarcraft.com/

Chapter 4
Design and Configuration of Firewall Architecture Under Risk, Usability and Cost Constraints

Abstract Firewalls are the most deployed security devices in computer networks. Nevertheless, designing and configuring distributed firewalls, which include determining access control rules and device placement in the network, is still a significantly complex task as it requires balancing between connectivity requirements and the inherent risk and cost. Formal approaches that allow for investigating distributed firewall configuration space systematically are highly needed to optimize decision support under multiple design constraints. The objective of this chapter is to automatically synthesize the implementation of distributed filtering architecture and configuration that will minimize security risk while considering connectivity requirements, user usability and budget constraints. Our automatic synthesis generates not only the complete rule configuration for each firewall to satisfy risk and connectivity constraints, but also the optimal firewall placement in the networks to minimizes spurious traffic. We define fine-grain risk, usability and cost metrics tunable to match business requirements, and formalize the configuration synthesis as an optimization problem. We then show that distributed firewall synthesis is an NP-hard problem and provide heuristic approximation algorithms. We implemented our approach in a tool called *FireBlanket* that were rigorously evaluated under different network sizes, topologies and budget requirements. Our evaluation study shows that the results obtained by *FireBlanket* are close to the theoretical lower bound and the performance is scalable with the network size.

4.1 Introduction

Designing a usable distributed filtering architecture and configurations requires careful balancing between number of competing factors: risk, usability satisfaction and cost. As filtering device configurations are hardened to reduce risk, it might be unnecessary too restrictive to achieve satisfiable usability or too expensive from budget or cost-benefit ratio perspective. Therefore, optimum usable security must provide satisfiable usability and minimum risk and cost. The enterprise security operations are mostly expert-based and ad-hoc, which might create instability and insecurity in enterprise networks.

The increasing complexity of designing and managing security configurations due to conflicting factors, larger networks, and longer policies makes configuration

© Springer International Publishing Switzerland 2014

E. Al-Shaer, *Automated Firewall Analytics: Design, Configuration and Optimization*, DOI 10.1007/978-3-319-10371-6_4

errors highly likely. Misconfigurations can cause reachability problems, security violations, and network vulnerabilities. Recent studies have found that more than 62 % of network failures today are due to network misconfiguration [4].

Recent research works focus on verifying and hardening network security configuration. For example, attack graphs creation and analysis to block attacks has been presented in various studies such as [9, 13, 16, 18]. Also, global security policies verification has been studied in [3, 4, 8, 14].

On the other hand, automatic synthesis of firewall configurations to generate a comprehensive distributed filtering architecture under competing design factors is still unaddressed problem. Reasoning about distributed filtering architecture and configuration in the context of risk, limiting spurious traffic, usability satisfaction, and business and budget requirements is a challenging problem. In this chapter, we first identify and formalize security configuration factors in order to quantify usability satisfaction, risk and cost. We then formulate the distributed firewall synthesis problem (DFSP) as an optimization problem. The solution of this problem determines: (1) the optimal locations of firewalls in the network to enforce polices while minimizing spurious traffic, (2) the correct firewall rules that satisfy system requirements while minimizing risk. We show that this problem is NP-hard and present greedy heuristics approximation algorithm that is accurate, scalable and practical. As a result, we present a holistic configuration approach to optimize distributed firewall architecture and configuration by automatically balancing usability satisfaction, risk and cost, while minimizing unwanted spurious traffic in the network. The resulting tool (FireBlanket) can be used as decision support tool to create distributed firewall architecture on clean-slate networks (assuming only connected hosts/services) or to refine existing firewall configurations.

The remainder of this chapter is organized as follows. In Sect. 4.2, we formalize the DFSP and show its complicity. We describe the approximation algorithm implemented in FireBlanket in Sect. 4.3. In Sect. 4.4, we evaluate the performance of FireBlanket through a set of simulation experiments and a real-life network case studies. The summary section is in Sects. 4.5.

4.2 System Model and Problem Formulation

We can define the firewall synthesis problem as follows: given the a network topology, deployed network services, business connectivity requirements ($\mathcal{Q}$), connectivity demand $\mathcal{D}$, usability profile S and cost c, the goal is to calculate the *minimum subset of firewalls* that can be places in various links and *subset of permitted flows* ($\mathcal{Q} \cup \mathcal{D}$) to minimize *risk (R)*, while satisfying the *connection requirements ($\mathcal{Q}$)*, the deployment *budget (B)* and *usability satisfaction (S)* and spurious traffic limitation constraints.

Table 4.1 Parameters and definitions in the model

Parameter	Definition
x_{mn}	Decision variable, represents whether link m,n has a firewall deployed.
V_i	The overall vulnerability of node i.
r_{ij}^g	The risk of flow from i to j for service g.
I_j	The impact if node j is comprised.
S_j	The usability satisfaction of node j.
w_{ij}^g	The importance of traffic between i and j for service g.
y_{ij}^g	Decision variable that represents whether traffic from node i to node j for service g is allowed. $y_{ij}^g = 1$ means allow.
f_{ij}^g	Service flow from node i to j for service g
q_{ij}^g	Connection requirement, represents whether the service flow from node i to j for service g should be allowed.
d_{ij}^g	Connection demand, represents the users's wish for the flow from i to j for service g, which can be denied for security consideration.
e_{mn}	is the cost of deploying a firewall on edge m,n.
B_{max}	Deployment budget threshold.
$\hat{S}_j$	Usability satisfaction threshold for node j.
o_{ij}^g	The distance the spurious traffic can travel from i to j before it is blocked.

4.2.1 Formal Problem Definition

We can represent a large-scale enterprise network as an undirected graph, $G(V;E)$, where V and $E \subseteq V \times V$ denote the set of nodes and links, respectively. A node in this model represents a logical unit (subnet) in the network, which can be one machine or a set of machines as long as all machines in that set share the same traffic flow and security properties. For example, the external network could be represented as one node or set of nodes based on the user classification of external nodes (the outside blacklisted hosts can collapse as one untrusted node). A *service flow* is a collection of packets that originate from one hots/service and terminate at another host/service. The leaf nodes in graph G usually represent servers, end hosts or subnets, and the core nodes usually represent routers. We summarize the important service flow and monitoring parameters in Table 4.1.

The solution to an FireBlanket problem consists of two parts, (1) a set of links $E' \in E$ at which to place a firewall and (2) the firewall configuration policies (e.g., which service flows are allowed) at each firewall. In determining the deployment of firewalls and the configuration at each firewall, we are interested in the tradeoff between the risk, the usability satisfaction and deployment cost. The FireBlanket problem can therefore be stated as follows:

Problem Definition. Given a network $G(V;E)$, a subset of connected nodes $V' \in V$ running network services, and a set of service flows F from $\mathscr{D}$, the **objective** is to determine (1) a subset of links $E' \in E$ on which to place firewall, and (2) a subset of service flows $F' \in F$ that are permitted in the network, **such that** the *risk* of these services is minimized, the *connection requirements*, the deployment *cost* and *usability satisfaction* constraints are satisfied.

One of the objectives in this work is to find the configuration, but not to optimize the configuration in deployed security devices. We want to find the correct configuration only. So, in this work, we only find the allowed flows (allow rules) for each firewall. Each allowed flow implies an allow rule in the firewalls deployed along the path of this flow. And we use the default deny everything rule to block the denied flow. Thus, the rule sets created for each firewall are anomaly free [3].

4.2.2 Metrics and Parameters for Design Synthesis

In our approach, the synthesis of the distributed security configuration is based on number of input parameters that are easy to obtain in practice. These parameters are defined in high-level specification and they include network topology, connectivity requirements, connectivity demands, and usability profiles.

The connectivity requirements ($\mathcal{Q}$) states (1) the required accessibility based on business mission (e.g., "the Web server can always be accessed via the Internet"), (2) service dependencies (e.g., "accessing the Web server requires accessing the DNS server"). The connectivity requirements must be satisfied by FireBlanket solution.

The connectivity demands ($\mathcal{D}$) represents all network flows the users wish to have besides the connection requirements. Unlike the connection requirements, some of the connectivity demands might be granted by FireBlanket based on security constraints. This means the connectivity demands are usually for non-critical network services (e.g., instant messaging). Therefore, allowing $\mathcal{D}$ connections will certainly improve user satisfaction, but denying them will not impact the business operation.

The usability profile ($\mathcal{S}$) is per user or class of users. It describes the services to be deployed and their priorities (i.e., ranking) from the user perspective. For example, for a student machine, Skype might be more important than Secure Shell (SSH), while it could be the opposite for a faculty machine. The user satisfaction in our system is computed based on usability profiles. The goal of FireBlanket is to satisfy the users' satisfaction constraints while minimizing the risk on the global system.

Both $\mathcal{Q}$, $\mathcal{D}$ and $\mathcal{S}$ can be created based on business policies, requirements and network service database, respectively. Moreover, the connection requirements and connection demands can also be defined by high level policy specification language similar as the language proposed in [1]. The budget is simply the maximum amount to be spent on firewall deployment, configuration and maintenance. For risk estimation, users will provide information about the critical assets on their network and the value of estimated damage. Using the estimated damage and service venerability score, risk can be estimated.

4.2.3 FireBlanket Framework

In this section, we describe our formulation for each factor considered in FireBlanket.

4.2.3.1 Formalization of Usability Satisfaction

Suppose there are G type of services in the network. Let f_{ij}^g represent the service flow from node i to node j for service $g \in G$. In FireBlanket, each end host j is associated with a usability profile. Each usability profile defines how many services are running at each host and the rank or importance of each service to that host. The higher the rank, the important the service is to the node. Let A_j^g denote the rank of service g in node j which is defined in usability profile, then the weight of service g (W_j^g) can be calculated by normalizing the rank value as follows:

$$W_j^g = \frac{A_j^g}{\sum_g A_j^g} \tag{4.1}$$

Each usability profile can further define the rank of each flow under each service. Let a_{ij}^g denotes the rank of flow f_{ij}^g in usability profile for service g at node j. The rank value a_{ij}^g can represent the address space of i (how many hosts in the virtual node i), the importance of source node i or the combination of these factors. For example, flows from larger subnet and more important source (the dean's office) should have higher ranking value. However, this can be customized to reflect the requirements of each individual user. Similarly, based on the rank value, the weight of this flow (w_{ij}^g) can be computed as follows:

$$w_{ij}^g = \frac{a_{ij}^g}{\sum_i a_{ij}^g} \tag{4.2}$$

For each service g running on node j, its service usability satisfaction decreases if service access is denied (e.g. firewall blocking traffic flows). Thus, we define the Service Usability Satisfaction (s_j^g) as the ratio of *granted* access (number of flows) by FireBlanket and the total *requested* access for service g of node j in the connectivity demands, $\mathcal{D}$. For instance, a service will have 100 % usability of it can be reached by all nodes as requested in $\mathcal{D}$. We use $d_{ij}^g \in \mathcal{D}$ (0 or 1) to indicates whether the traffic flow of service g from node i to j is *demanded* in $\mathcal{D}$. We also use y_{ij}^g as decision variables to indicates whether the service flow from node i to j is *allowed* (via firewalls) by FireBlanket. We can compute the Service Usability Satisfaction (s_j^g) as follows:

$$s_j^g = \frac{\sum_i y_{ij}^g w_{ij}^g}{\sum_i d_{ij}^g w_{ij}^g} \qquad (4.3)$$

Based to the individual service usability satisfaction, we can calculate the overall service usability satisfaction (S_j) of node j, which is the weighted summation of service usability satisfaction of each service:

$$S_j = \sum_g W_j^g s_j^g \qquad (4.4)$$

4.2.3.2 Formalization of Security Risk

Risk has many contributing factors and it is sometimes infeasible to consider all of them simultaneously. However, minimizing any subset of these factors can improve security significantly. In our previous work [11], we consider service vulnerability based on history. There are several works have been proposed in the area of risk assessment [6, 11]. In this work, we present a risk metric using well-known factors: (1) the potential damage, I_j, when node j is compromised, (2) the overall vulnerability (V_i) of source node i and (3) the vulnerability of service g at node j (v_j^g). I_j can be estimated from business mission. The individual service vulnerability v_j^g comes from Common Vulnerability Scoring System (CVSS) [15], which provides scores in the range 1–10, where the higher the value, the severe the vulnerability. The overall vulnerability V_i equals the maximal vulnerability of running service on node i, $V_i = max_g(v_i^g)$.

We can compute the potential damage node i can cause to node j $(\hat{r}_{ij}^g)$ due to attack on node j through service g if node i is compromised. Here, $\hat{r}_{ij}^g = V_i v_j^g I_j$. The risk implies by a traffic flow is proportional with the overall vulnerability of source node (V_i) and the destination service vulnerability (v_j^g). Intuitively, V_i represents how possible attack can be originated from node i, and v_j^g represents how possible the attack can succeed at node j running service g. After firewall deployment, the residual risk (r_{ij}^g) can be defined as follows:

$$r_{ij}^g = V_i v_j^g I_j y_{ij}^g \qquad (4.5)$$

In the rest of this chapter, risk always means residual risk. Consequently, the aggregated risk on node j can be computed as:

$$R_j = max_{i,g}(r_{ij}^g) \qquad (4.6)$$

4.2.3.3 Formalization of Deployment Cost

Deploying firewall at network link $\{m,n\}$ associates with a deployment cost c_{mn}, which can be computed as follows:

$$c_{mn} = x_{mn} e_{mn} \tag{4.7}$$

Here the decision variable x_{mn} represents whether there is a firewall deployed on link $\{m,n\}$, where $x_{mn} = 1$ means there is a firewall on link $\{m,n\}$. And e_{mn} stands for the cost of deploying a firewall on link $\{m,n\}$ which can be calculated based on device price, hardware installation and software configuration. Based on the network topology and traffic throughput, different firewalls may be deployed on different links. For example, backbone link should be deployed with enterprise level firewall. On the contrary, the end-user machines should be deployed with host-based firewall.

4.2.3.4 Formalization of Spurious Traffic

Spurious traffic refers to the traffic flow which travel portions of the its path to the destination before it is blocked by a firewall. Spurious traffic consumes network bandwidth and increase the network vulnerability to deny of service (DOS) and other possible attacks embedded in spurious traffic. Ideally, unwanted traffic should not be allowed to get into the network. But in practice, it is impossible to have firewall deployed everywhere. Thus, we need limit amount of spurious traffics in the network. In this work, we control limit the amount of spurious traffic by controlling the distance (hops) that the spurious traffic can travel in the network. We use o_{ij}^g to represent the distance that the spurious traffic can travel from node i to j of service g before it gets blocked by a firewall. We use P_{ij} to represent the set of links from node i to j.

$$P_{ij} = \{p_{ij}^1, p_{ij}^2, \ldots, p_{ij}^{M_{ij}}\} \tag{4.8}$$

where p_{ij}^τ represent the τth link along the path from node i to j. So o_{ij}^g can be get as follows:

$$o_{ij}^g = (1 - y_{ij}^g) \sum_{h=1}^{M_{ij}} \prod_{\tau=1}^{h} (1 - x_{p_{ij}^\tau}) \tag{4.9}$$

From Eq. (4.9) we can see that o_{ij}^g is calculated by counting how many links the flow can travel before it is blocked by the first firewall along the path. Here, $x_{p_{ij}^\tau}$ represents whether the τth link along the path from i to j has firewall deployed.

4.2.3.5 Usability Satisfaction Control

FireBlanket allows the administrator to control the usability satisfaction at three levels. The most fine-grained usability satisfaction can be achieved by defining the individual threshold $(\hat{S}_j)$ for each node/user, $S_j \geq \hat{S}_j$. Based on the role (obligation and functionality) of each user in the organization, the users (service nodes) can be classified into different groups (e.g., faculties, students). Let N_l represents the set of nodes in group l, the administrator can define the service satisfaction threshold $(\hat{S}_{N_l})$ for the minimal usability satisfaction of group l. More generally, the usability satisfaction can be controlled globally across the network by defining threshold $(\hat{S}_{global})$, which is the minimal usability satisfaction for every node. Using these three levels of control, administrators can fine tune the FireBlanket with great flexibility to achieve desired security configuration.

4.2.3.6 Formalization of FireBlanket Optimization Problem

Let B_{max} denotes the deployment budget, and $\hat{R}_j$ represents the risk threshold for node j, we can then formalize the FireBlanket Synthesis Problem as follows:

$$minimize \sum_i \sum_j \sum_g r_{ij}^g \tag{4.10}$$

subject to

$$S_j \geq \hat{S}_j \tag{4.11}$$

$$S_j \geq \hat{S}_{N_l} \ j \in N_l \tag{4.12}$$

$$S_j \geq \hat{S}_{global} \tag{4.13}$$

$$r_{ij}^g \leq \hat{R}_j, \forall \, i, j \tag{4.14}$$

$$\sum_{mn} c_{mn} < B_{max} \tag{4.15}$$

$$y_{ij}^g \geq q_{ij}^g \tag{4.16}$$

$$o_{ij}^g \leq T \tag{4.17}$$

$$\sum_{\{m,n\} \in P_{ij}} x_{mn} \geq 1 - y_{ij}^g \ for \ d_{ij}^g = 1 \tag{4.18}$$

Let q_{ij} denotes the connection and security requirements, $q_{ij} = 1$ means service flow from node i must reach node j. Note that satisfying the Connection Requirements avoids unrealistic solutions of FireBlanket synthesis problem such as blocking connection to/from the Internet. The usability satisfaction for individual users, group of users and all users are defined in Eqs. (4.11)–(4.13). The cost of deployment firewalls should be less than the deployment budget, which is shown in Eq. (4.15). Connection requirements are satisfied by Eq. (4.16). Spurious traffic is controlled by Eq. (4.17), T is the maximal hops spurious traffic can travel. And Eq. (4.18) links decision variable x_{mn} and y_{ij} together which means if traffic between i and j is blocked, then there must be at least one firewall deployed in the path from i to j. Additionally, the user can also define thresholds for many different groups or global minimal usability satisfaction.

4.2.4 Computational Complexity

Theorem 4.1. *The optimal distributed filtering architecture and configuration problem (DFSP) is a NP-hard problem.*

Proof. The DFSP problem is proven to be NP-hard via a reduction from the knapsack problem [17], which is stated as follows. Given a set of n items, each represented by its volume V_i and price P_i and a knapsack with maximal carrying weight T_{max}, find a set of items with total weight at most T_{max} with maximum possible price. Considering a simplified DFSP problem by relaxing the deployment budget constraint. Then, the problem is to find the subset of service flows to be denied in the network to achieve minimal residual risk (maximal risk reduction) and satisfy usability satisfaction threshold. e can see that minimal global risk can be achieved by minimizing risk for each service, which is the sub problem of the original DFSP problem, we call it SDFSP problem. Given an instance of the knapsack problem, we create an instance of SDFSP problem as follows. First we create a create a bipartite graph G_B, each item i in knapsack instance with volume V_i and price P_i corresponds to one node m_i in one side of bipartite graph. Then we create a service node s in other side of the bipartite graph. We create a service flow between s and each node m_i with weight $w_{si} = P_i$. We set the impact of each node equal the volume of each item, $I_i = V_i$. Then we set the connection demand $d_{si} = 1$ and connection requirement $q_{si} = 0$. The UST reduction threshold $(1 - \hat{S}_j)$ is equal T_{max}. Clearly, through this reduction we can see that there exists a solution of total risk reduction K to the given SDFSP problem if and only if there exists a solution of total price K to the Knapsack problem.

4.2.5 Demilitarized Zones Creation

The distributed filtering architecture (configuration rules and device placement) are created based on existing network topology. However, due to the budget limitation and network topology restriction, the solutions generated by FireBlanket may not provide adequate isolation of service nodes. There may exist the situation that one node can reach the service on other nodes even these connections are not in connectivity demands. This is because the budget does not allow FireBlanket to place firewall to block these connections. Thus, we propose an automated technique to create internal and external demilitarized zone (DMZ) for each firewall based on rules by FireBlanket and services requirements. A DMZ is a physical or logical subnetwork that contains services (hosts) that are exposed to untrusted or less secure networks [12]. The cascading multiple DMZs in a network is shown in Fig. 4.1. DMZ improves network security by increasing network isolation and enforcing defense-in-depth. In this model, each firewall fw_k has three interfaces: outside, inside and DMZ. Each interface directly connects with one zone (area): secure zone (Z_k), less-secure zone (Z_{k-1}) and DMZ (dmz_k). Each zone in this approach is a set of nodes which can communicate with each other without filtering devices control. The security levels of these three zones in descending order are Z_k, DMZ_k and Z_{k-1}. DMZ_1 is usually called public DMZ while $DMZ_k (k > 1)$ are usually called internal DMZs [12]. The traffic pattern between these zones is as follows: Outside can accesses DMZ, but not inside secure network; DMZ can accesses outside and limited machines in inside secure network (e.g., RADIUS server); Inside secure network can accesses DMZ and outside network.

The DMZ is created by transferring nodes from inside zone to DMZ if their traffic pattern fit in DMZ. Formally, we have following definition:

Definition 4.1. A DMZ area, DMZ_k, of firewall fw_k is a subnet that contains hosts such that these hosts can be reached from an external zones (Z_h) that exhibits weaker security (or higher risk), and they can only initiate communication to the limited hosts in secure zone Z_k.

Without loosing generality, we assume the index of security zone reflects zone security level. Zone Z_k is more secure than zone Z_{k-1}. Let H_s represent the set of special hosts which allow access from less secure zone (DMZ) based on business requirements. Based on this definition, we can identify nodes which belong to DMZ_k as below:

Definition 4.2. A host i is assigned to DMZ_k iff (1) host i accept traffic from zone Z_{k-1} and possibly from zone Z_p where $p > k$, and (2) host i can only initiate communication with limited hosts j in zone Z_p where $p \geq k$ and $j \in H_s$.

Let us assume P_k is the accept policy of fw_k as defined in [8]. For the secure zone Z_k, F_{ext}^k is a Boolean expression that represents flows coming from less-secure zones (external) to Z_k, and F_{int}^k is a Boolean expression that represents flows going from host in a secure zone to another host in the same secure zone (internal) but not in H_s. These two set of flows can be defined as follows:

$$F_{ext}^k = \bigvee_{\forall i \in Z_k, j \in Z_p, p < k} [IPsrc = IP(j) \wedge IPdest = IP(i)] \qquad (4.19)$$

$$F_{int}^k = \bigvee_{\forall i \in Z_k, j \in Z_k \setminus H_s} [IPsrc = IP(i) \wedge IPdest = IP(j)] \qquad (4.20)$$

Since FireBlanket generates policy P_k for each firewall fw_k, We can get the flows (ϕ_{ext}^k) that are allowed by the firewall fw_k to the secure zone Z_k coming from external less-secure zones. Flows (ϕ_{int}^k)that goes between hosts in the same secure zone can be identified in the same way based on connectivity demands D_k, which is the connectivity demands related to nodes in zone Z_k.

$$\phi_{ext}^k \leftarrow [P_k \wedge F_{ext}^k] \tag{4.21}$$

$$\phi_{int}^k \leftarrow [D_k \wedge F_{int}^k] \tag{4.22}$$

Based on these two set of flows, we can get the nodes (φ_k) belong to DMZ_k, which are the nodes accept flows from less secure zone Z_{k-1}, and do not initiate flows to nodes in $Z_k \setminus H_s$.

$$\varphi_k \leftarrow [\phi_{ext}^k(dst) \wedge \neg \phi_{int}^k(src)] \tag{4.23}$$

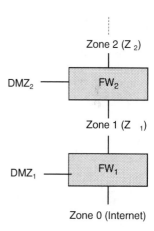

Fig. 4.1 Multiple cascading DMZs in a network

Algorithm 7 Heuristic greedy algorithm for DFSP

1: **for** $f_{ij}^g \in F$ **do**
2:      $\bar{s}_{ij}^g == W_j^g \frac{w_{ij}^g}{\sum_i d_{ij}^g w_{ij}^g}$
3:      $r_{ij}^g = V_i v_j^g I_j y_{ij}^g$
4: **end for**
5: $F_D \leftarrow getMinRiskFlows$
6: $L \leftarrow \emptyset$
7: $E' \leftarrow \emptyset$
8: **for** $f_{ij} \in F_D$ **do**
9:      **if** for edge$\{m,n\}$, $dist(in) < T$ **then**
10:          $E' \leftarrow E' \cup \{m,n\}$
11:      **end if**
12: **end for**
13: **while** $F_D \neq \emptyset$ **do**
14:      choose $l \in E'$ which can maximize $\frac{|f_l \setminus F_B|}{e_l}$
15:      $F_D \leftarrow F_D \setminus f_l$
16:      $L \leftarrow L \cup l$
17:      $E' \leftarrow E' \setminus l$
18: **end while**
19: **return** $L, F \setminus F_D$

4.3   Heuristic Algorithms

In this section, we propose a greedy heuristic algorithm to DFSP which is efficient and practical to implement in large-scale network. The algorithm take the network topology, connectivity demands, vulnerability of each service and overall vulnerability of each node, deployment budget and usability satisfaction threshold as input, output the link for firewall deployment and the service flows which should be allowed. Algorithm 7 illustrates our greedy algorithm. This algorithm solves the DFSP in three steps.

4.3.1   Heuristic Algorithm for DFSP

4.3.1.1   Step 1, Preprocessing

Each service flow f_{ij}^g has its contribution to the overall usability satisfaction of node j, represented by $\bar{s}_{ij}^g$. Based on the definition in Sect. 4.2.1, $\bar{s}_{ij}^g$ can be calculated by:

$$\bar{s}_{ij}^g = W_j^g \frac{w_{ij}^g}{\sum_i d_{ij}^g w_{ij}^g} \tag{4.24}$$

Algorithm 8 Heuristic algorithm for minimal risk flows selection: getMinRisk-Flows

---
1: $F_D \leftarrow \emptyset$
2: **for** Each node j **do**
3:    **if** No individual UST **then**
4:       **if** No group and global UST **then**
5:          $\hat{S}_j \leftarrow NULL$
6:       **else if** No Group UST **then**
7:          $\hat{S}_j \leftarrow \hat{S}_{N_l}$
8:       **else**
9:          $\hat{S}_j \leftarrow \hat{S}_{global}$
10:      **end if**
11:   **end if**
12:   $F_j^D \leftarrow \emptyset$
13:   $S_j \leftarrow 0$
14:   sort r_{ij}^g in descending order
15:   **while** $S_j < 1 - \hat{S}_j$ **do**
16:      select top flow f_{ij}^g in the list
17:      $F_j^D \leftarrow F_j^D \cup f_{ij}$
18:      $S_j \leftarrow S_j + \bar{s}_{ij}^g$
19:   **end while**
20:   $F_D \leftarrow F_j^D \cup F_D$
21: **end for**
22: return F_D

This algorithm first calculates $\bar{s}_{ij}^g$ and risk r_{ij}^g for each service flow (lines 1–4). Then, it will process the usability satisfaction thresholds (UST) (individual, group and global) provided by the user. The priorities of these thresholds in descending order are individual, group, global.

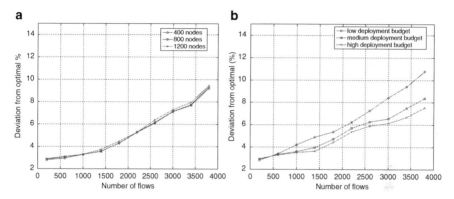

Fig. 4.2 Heuristic algorithm accuracy versus number of flows, the impact of network size and deployment budget on accuracy. (**a**) Network size; (**b**) deployment budget

4.3.1.2 Step 2, Minimal Risk Flows Selection

In this step, the algorithm greedily selects the subset of service flows to be allowed in the network based on the UST. Let F_j^A denote the subset of service flows which will be allowed in the network to achieve minimal risk under usability satisfaction threshold for node j, F_j^D represents the denied subset of flows. Select allowed flows to satisfy the UST and achieve minimal risk is equal to select denied flows to achieve maximal risk reduction and not violating UST. Thus, for each node, if UST exists, this algorithm sorts all service flows of this node based on their risk in descending order. Then it selects the first service flow from the flow list until there is no room for more flow to be blocked, which means

$$\sum_{f_{ij}^g \in F_j^D} \bar{s}_{ij}^g < 1 - \hat{S}_j \tag{4.25}$$

The algorithm for minimal risk flows selection is shown in Algorithm 8.

Algorithm 9 Incremental optimization

1: calculate s_{ij}^g, r_{ij}^g for $f_{ij}^g \in F_{new}$
2: $F_D \leftarrow getMinRiskFlows(F_{new}, s_{ij}^g, r_{ij}^g)$
3: $F_B \leftarrow \emptyset$
4: **for** each flow f_{ij}^g F_D **do**
5:     **if** $\sum_{\{m,n\} \in P_{ij}^g} x_{mn} \geq 1 - y_{ij}^g$ **then**
6:         $F_B \leftarrow F_B \cup f_l$
7:     **end if**
8: **end for**
9: **if** $F_D = F_B$ **then**
10:     update firewall policy based on F_D
11: **else**
12:     $F'_{new} \leftarrow F_D \backslash F_B$
13:     deploy new firewalls based on F'_{new} and current budget
14: **end if**

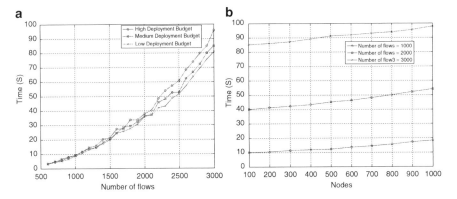

Fig. 4.3 FireBlanket performance, the impact of firewall deployment budget and network size on finishing time. (**a**) Deployment budget; (**b**) network size

4.3.1.3   Step 3, Firewall Deployment

The problem of finding the subset of links to deploy firewalls which can cover all the flows to be blocked under given budget constraints can be proven to be NP-hard by the directly mapping from the minimum weighted hitting set problem [2]. Our approximation algorithm selects the link which has the maximal ratio of new cover flows over deployment cost at each step until all denied flows have been covered or deployment budget has been reached.

4.3.2 Incremental Design Synthesis

In previous section, we assume the service flows and connection requirements are all given at once and we also assume that there are no firewalls deployed in the network. We can use FireBlanket to build the security architecture from scratch, and to find the best device deployment and configuration. But in real network environment, the service flows can dynamically change. For example, new flows can be added as a result of business development. The heuristic algorithm proposed in previous section can handle incremental updating with simple modification. The algorithm is shown in Algorithm 9. The intuition is to first identify the new flows need to be blocked for each node to achieve maximal risk reduction without violating the useability satisfaction threshold. Then, if current firewall deployment can block all those flows, we just update the configuration for each firewall. If not, we will deploy new firewalls based on the remaining budget to block those flows which can not be covered by current firewalls.

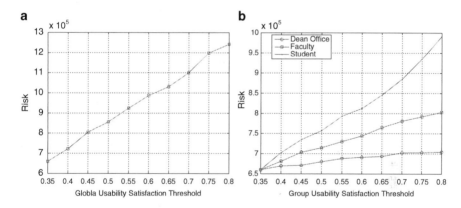

Fig. 4.4 The impact of UST to risk. (**a**) Global UST; (**b**) group UST

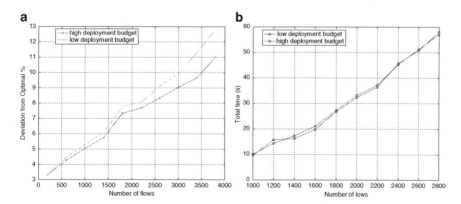

Fig. 4.5 Heuristic algorithm performance under incremental flow updating, the deviation from lower bound versus number of flows and the total time needed versus number of flows. (**a**) Deviation from lower bound; (**b**) total time needed

4.4   Evaluation

In this section, we evaluate FireBlanket using both simulation and real case studies. First, we conducted many simulation experiments to evaluate the accuracy and scalability of our approximation algorithms with respect to the optimal solutions. To evaluate the performance of FireBlanket under real-life network environment, we uses FireBlanket to analyze the campus network for an academic institution and generate the security configurations under different budgets and UST.

4.4.1   Accuracy and Scalability of the Heuristic Algorithm

Since our integer programming solver could not compute the optimal solutions for the large-size network, we use the LP relaxation of our problem to compute a crude lower bound on the optimal solution. The LP solution can be computed in reasonable time for relatively large networks by using MATLAB [10]. We conducted the experiments under different network sizes and service flow configurations with different firewall deployment budgets. We used GT-ITM [7] generate network topologies. Unfortunately, the GT-ITM topology does not provide traffic demand matrices for each topology generated. Therefore, we used the technique proposed in [5] to generate service flows. In these experiments, we assume each note has one service running. The service vulnerability is randomly assigned, $[1, 10]$. The impact for each end node is randomly selected from range 1 to 100. In the first set of experiments, we study the accuracy (deviation from optimal) of our approach as the number of service flows increases. The deviation is calculated as follows deviation $= \frac{optimal - heuristic}{optimal}\%$ We fix the network size (1,000 end hosts) and topology, but change the number of demanded service flows from 200 to 3,800. We limit the connectivity requirements to be maximum 10 % of the service flows. The deployment budget is the fixed maximal value of device deployment. But the actual deployment cost is determined by the FireBlanket solutions. We should guarantee that every denied flow has one firewall on its path, and the total cost of all firewalls can not be larger than budget. In order to eliminate the impact of the firewall deployment budget on accuracy, we adopt high deployment budget which means we can deploy firewalls to block every service flow. In this experiment, we only set the global UST to be 0.4, without setting group and individual UST. The results in Fig. 4.2a show that the deviation from the lower bound slightly increases as the number of flows increases. But the deviation ratio is less than 10 % for a reasonable large number of service flows. Also the accuracy of our algorithm almost remains constant as the network size changes. This is because our algorithm attempts to select the subset of flows that minimizes the risk, no matter if these flows running on small or large networks. Thus, the number of flows dominates the impact on performance.

In the next set of experiments, we study the impact of deployment budget on the accuracy of our heuristic. For each network topology, we fix the global UST, and flow configuration. We also change the firewall deployment budget levels: low,

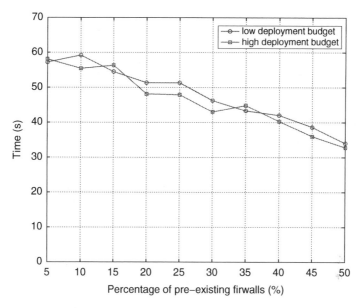

Fig. 4.6 Completion time versus pre-existing firewalls

medium and high. The high deployment budget means for current network topology and service flows, we can deploy firewall to block all service flows. Medium budget means around 10 % of the service flows will not be filtered by firewall under any deployment plan based on the budgets. Low budget means 30 % of the flows are not filtered by firewalls. We evaluate how our proposed heuristic performs under various service flows configuration ranging from 200 to 3,800. The result in Fig. 4.2b show that low deployment budget can increase the deviation because our heuristic approach allows a set of flows, which should be denied, to transfer on the network due to low deployment budget.

In the third set of experiments, we study the scalability of our greedy heuristic algorithm. We implement FireBlanket using java and conduct the experiments on one PC with P4 2.4G cpu with 2 GB memory. We conduct the experiments in a network with 1,000 nodes. To study the impact of deployment budget, we fix the global UST and change the deployment budget in three different levels: Low, Medium, High. Figure 4.3a shows the algorithm completion time as the number of network flows change. We can see that increasing the firewall deployment budget does not have much impact on algorithm completion time. And as the number of service flow increases, the algorithm can still run in reasonable time. In the fourth set of experiments, we evaluate the impact of network size on completion time. For each network topology, we have three service flow configurations 1,000, 2,000 and 3,000. We change the network size from 100 to 1,000 end hosts. The result in Fig. 4.3b show that the execution time varies from few to 90 s which is practically a reasonable figure.

4.4.2   A Case Study

We use the network of an academic institution as case study. This network is composed of 12 different subnets and 341 end host machines for faculties, staffs, and students. Based on the importance, responsibility and activity, these 341 end hosts are divided into 11 groups including: faculty, student, research lab, general staff, administrator, dean office, etc. The impact of each host is assigned based on its importance ranging from 1 to 100. We consider 15 common network services in this study and use the base score from CVSS as the vulnerability for each service. The connectivity requirements and demands are generated based on teaching and research activity. We first study the impact of different level of usability satisfaction threshold to the global risk. We set firewall deployment budget high to minimize its impact. We first study the impact of global UST (without group and individual UST) by increasing its value from 0.3 to 0.8 with an increase step of 0.05. The results in Fig. 4.4a show that the global risk increases as the global UST increases. Since the connectivity requirements must be satisfied, such connections represent the minimal risk and usability value in the system. This is the starting point of the curve in Fig. 4.4a. We test the impact of group UST to the risk by selecting three groups: faculty, student and dean office. We set the global UST = 0.3 and change the each group UST from 0.3 to 0.8. The results in Fig. 4.4b show that adjusting the UST for different groups has different impact on the global risk. Also, increasing the student usability satisfaction will greatly increase the risk because students demand high risk services such as P2P file sharing, instant messaging with untrusted sites.

   In order to evaluate the distributed firewall architecture provided by FireBlanket, we use FireBlanket to generate distributed filtering architecture under different budgets for testing networks while maintaining the usability satisfaction as the same as in the current configurations. We then generate the attack graphs [16] for both the current real network and FireBlanket configuration. We identify and compare the attack scenarios to compromise several critical assets in both the current and FireBlanket architecture. The results in Table 4.2 show that FireBlanket reduces the risk significantly by eliminating more than 75 % of the attacks scenarios. It also shows that reducing budget might increase risk (attacks) but increasing it may not always result in reducing risk.

4.4.3   Incremental Updating

In this experiments, we study the accuracy and scalability of the incremental updating algorithm discussed in Sect. 4.3.2. We set the number of initial flows as 1,000 in a fixed network with 1,000 nodes. Then we gradually added more flows. We compare the result from the incremental updating algorithm with the result generated by LP solver using complete flow set as input. The result is shown in Fig. 4.5a. We can see that when number of flows increases from 1,000 to 2,800, the deviation from the lower bound increases from 3.4 to 12.8 %. The change of finishing time versus the incremental flow updating is shown in Fig. 4.5b. Clearly, the finishing time increases slowly as the number of flows increase. And the deployment budget has no obvious impact on finishing time. We also study the performance of FireBlanket when pre-existing firewalls are already deployed in the network. The percentage of the pre-existing firewalls changes from 5 to 50 % of the total deployed firewalls. The change of finishing time as the percentage of pre-existing firewall increases is shown in Fig. 4.6. We can see that the finishing time decrease slowly from 58 to 32 s as the percentage of pre-existing firewalls increase from 5 to 50 %.

4.5 Summary

Automating design synthesis of firewall configuration is one of the main standing challenges in today's networks. The manual or ad hoc design and configuration of networks does not only causes serious misconfigurations but it also does not allow for evaluating alternative configurations systemically for provable security. Furthermore, the complexity of distributed security configuration synthesis increases significantly as multiple contradicting constraints such as risk, usability satisfaction and cost are to be considered.

To the best of our knowledge, this work is the first approach to optimize distributed firewall architecture systematically, automate rules configuration synthesis and evaluate configuration alternatives quantitatively. The proposed system, called FireBlanket, determines the firewalls placement and rules to minimize risk while enforcing connection requirements, usability, cost and spurious traffic constraints. We formulate (1) *risk* based on potential propagation of infection, (2) *usability* based on user demand and satisfaction, and (3) *cost* based on deployment effort and then formulate the firewall synthesis problem as an IP optimization problem. We prove that firewall synthesis problem is NP-hard by a reduction from Kanpsack problem. We presented a greedy approximation algorithm for firewall synthesis and conducted rigorous evaluation experiments using both simulation and real-life case studies. Our evaluation study shows that our greedy approximation algorithm deviates from the lower bound by maximum 12 %, even with large size network of 1,000 end-hosts with 4,000 network flows. We also show that the execution time is between order of seconds to few minutes for more than 1,000 of end-hosts and many thousands of simultaneous flows.

Table 4.2 Comparison of attack scenarios between existing architecture and FireBlanket architecture

Distributed filtering architecture	Attack scenarios
Current network	128
FireBlanket (current budget)	31
FireBlanket (90 % of current budget)	40
FireBlanket (110 % of current budget)	17
FireBlanket (120 % of current budget)	17

References

1. Bin Zhang, Ehab Al-Shaer, Radha Jagadeesan, James Riely, and Corin Pitcher. Specifications of a high-level conflict-free firewall policy language for multi-domain networks. In Proceedings of 12th ACM Symposium on Access Control Models And Technologies (SACMAT), June 20–22, 2007.
2. A. Cincotti, V. Cutello, and F. Pappalardo. An ant-algorithm for the weighted minimum hitting set problem. Swarm Intelligence Symposium, 2003.
3. Ehab Al-Shaer, Hazem Hamed, Raouf Boutaba, and Masum Hasan. Conflict classification and analysis of distributed firewall policies. In IEEE Journal on Selected Areas in Communications (JSAC), 2005.
4. Ehab Al-shaer, Wilfredo Marrero, Adel El-atawy, and Khalid Elbadawi. Network configuration in a box: Towards end-to-end verification of network reachability and security. In *International Conference on Network Protocols*, pages 123–132, 2009.
5. B. Fortz and M. Thorup. Internet traffic engineering by optimizing ospf weights. Proc. IEEE INFOCOM, 2000.
6. A.K. Ganame and J. Bourgeois. Defining a simple metric for real-time security level evaluation of multi-sites networks. 4th int. Workshop on Security in Systems and Networks (colloaed with IPDPS'08), 2008.
7. Georgia Tech. Modeling topology of large internetworks. http://www.cc.gatch.edu/fac/Ellen.Zegura/graphs.html.
8. Hazem Hamed, Ehab Al-Shaer, and Will Marrero. Modeling and verification of ipsec and vpn security policies. in Proceedings of IEEE ICNP'2005, November 2005.
9. John Homer and Xinming Ou. Sat-solving approaches to context-aware enterprise network security management. In IEEE JSAC Special Issue on Network Infrastructure Configuration, To appear.
10. Matlab. Mathworks. http://www.mathworks.com/.
11. Mohamed Salim, Ehab Al-Shaer, and Latifur Khan. Integrated risk evaluation for automated security management. Journal of Network and System Management (JNSM), to appear, 2011.
12. Nist guidelines on firewalls and firewall policy. http://csrc.nist.gov/publications/nistpubs/800-41/sp800-41.pdf.
13. Rinku Dewri, Nayot Poolsappasit Indrajit Ray, and Darrell Whitley. Optimal security hardening using multi-objective optimization on attack tree models of networks. Proceedings of the 14th ACM conference on Computer and communications security, 2007.
14. Sanjai Narain, Gary Levin, Vikram Kaul, and Sharad Malik. Declarative infrastructure configuration synthesis and debugging. Journal of Network and Systems Management, 2008.
15. M. Schiffman. A complete guide to the common vulnerability scoring system (cvss). http://www.first.org/cvss/cvss-guide.html, 2009.
16. O. Sheyner, J. Haines, S. Jha, R. Lippmann, and J. M. Wing. Automated generation and analysis of attack graphs. Proceedings of the IEEE Symposium on Security and Privacy, 2002.
17. Silvano Martello and Paolo Toth. *Knapsack Problems: Algorithms and Computer Implementations*. John Wiley & Sons. ISBN 0-471-92420-2., 1990.
18. Xinming Ou, Wayne F. Boyer, and Miles A. McQueen. A scalable approach to attack graph generation. In *13th ACM Conference on Computer and Communications Security*, 2006.

Chapter 5
Dynamic Firewall Configuration Optimization

Abstract Security policies play a critical role in many of the current network security technologies such as firewalls, IPSec and IDS devices. The configuration of these policies not only determines the functionality of such devices, but also substantially affects their performance. The optimization of filtering policy configuration is critically important to provide high performance packet filtering particularly for firewalls. Current packet filtering techniques exploit the characteristics of the filtering policies, but they do not consider the traffic behavior in optimizing their search data structures. This often results in high space complexity, which undermines the performance gain offered by these techniques. Also, these techniques offer upper bounds for the worst case search times; nevertheless, the more common average case scenarios are not necessarily optimized.

In this chapter, we first classify, describe and compare the existing dynamic firewall policy configuration techniques based on-line and off-line traffic analysis.

Second, we present a novel technique that utilizes Internet traffic characteristics to dynamically optimize the rule ordering (DRO) of firewall policies dynamically. The proposed technique timely adapts to the traffic conditions using actively calculated statistics to dynamically optimize the ordering of packet filtering rules. The rule importance in traffic matching as well as its dependency on other rules are both considered in our optimization algorithm. Through extensive evaluation experiments using simulated and real Internet traffic traces, the proposed mechanism is shown to be efficient and easy to deploy in practical firewall implementations.

5.1 Introduction

Security technologies like Firewalls, IPSec and IDS have become major components in the current high speed Internet infrastructure to filter out undesired traffic and protect the integrity and confidentiality of critical traffic. In these devices, the filtering decision is based on a *filtering security policy* designed according to predefined high level security requirements and is composed of a number of ordered filtering rules against which the network traffic is sequentially matched in order to determine the appropriate filtering action. Therefore, packet filtering is a critical component that consumes a significant amount of processing power and greatly impacts the performance of these networking devices. With the dramatic advances

© Springer International Publishing Switzerland 2014   95
E. Al-Shaer, *Automated Firewall Analytics: Design, Configuration
and Optimization*, DOI 10.1007/978-3-319-10371-6_5

in the current network speeds, firewall packet filtering must be constantly optimized to cope with the network traffic demands and attacks. This requires reducing the packet matching time needed to "permit" or "deny" packets in order to minimize the end-to-end delay. This problem is even more critical in application-level filtering, where various types of network, transport and application layer packet header fields are used to filter traffic. Thus, efficient yet easy to implement optimization of filtering policies is highly crucial to enable high speed packet filtering for effective deployment of traffic filtering technologies in the Internet.

Our work in this chapter is highly motivated by a number of Internet traffic properties that we observed in our study and addressed by other researchers [8, 19] as well. Our study of many Internet and private packet traces shows that the major portion of the network traffic matches a small subset of the firewall rules. We also observed that this "skewness" in traffic distribution over policy rules is likely to stay for time intervals that are sufficient to make such skewness important to consider in packet filtering. In this chapter, we show that the rule ordering optimization problem with rule dependency constraints is NP-complete, and we present a novel *dynamic rule ordering technique* that employs the matching skewness of firewall rules to enhance filtering performance. Our ordering scheme splits the filtering policy into two layers of rules. The top layer consists of a small set of the most *active rules* (i.e., currently performs the most packet matching) ordered based on their traffic matching contribution in order to minimize the overall packet matching. The second layer usually contains a larger set of the remaining *inactive rules* that performs much less matching. The performance of the optimized policy is constantly monitored and the rule ordering is automatically updated in order to adapt to any new traffic statistics. Our technique exhibits lightweight implementation and can be easily generalized for other filtering devices operating at higher levels of the network stack such as Intrusion Detection/Prevention Systems.

Packet filtering policy optimization has been studied extensively in the research literature [12]. However, many of the current packet classification techniques exploit the characteristics of filtering rules but they do not consider the traffic behavior in their optimization schemes. Being deterministic, these techniques guarantee an upper bound on the packet matching time, but may not provide optimized average case performance. On the other hand, our statistical matching approach aims to improve the average filtering time. In addition, unlike many of the presented techniques, our technique has much less space complexity and can be used with any filtering rule formats including application-level filtering policies. The use of statistical structures for optimizing routing table lookups was discussed in [13]. However, the proposed technique uses only a single field (routing prefix) that has a given packet hit frequency distribution. Optimization of decision lists has been briefly discussed in [8]. The work was mainly focused on optimizing the space complexity of packet filtering decision trees, and used a simple greedy algorithm for ordering filtering rules as one step in the approach. However, the greedy algorithm works only when most of the filtering rules are disjoint. None of these techniques explain how to maintain the traffic statistics or how the optimizations can be efficiently integrated in the packet filtering process.

In the first part of this chapter, we present a classification study and comparison of dynamic firewall configuration techniques based on their goals, schemes, complexity, applicability and limitations. We classify dynamic firewall optimization techniques into two categories based on their goals: *matching optimization* and *early rejection optimization* schemes. Matching optimization techniques try to minimize the matching time of normal network traffic. Early rejection techniques create a minimum set of a policy preamble rules (constraints) that can potentially filter out the maximum amount of denied traffic. Both categories are self-adaptive to ensure that the performance gain will always supersede the dynamic management maintenance overhead. We believe that our work provides important insights on the operation and use of traffic-aware filtering.

In the second part of this chapter, we selected the dynamic rule ordering (DRO) as the most practical dynamic configuration optimization technique that requires no policy transformation or hardware adaptation. DRO can statistically optimize the order of access control list incorporating any filtering field type, and update the rule order based on real-time network traffic statistics.

The chapter is organized as follows. Section 5.2 presents the background and definitions related to firewall packet filtering. Section 5.3 describes the motivation for dynamic firewall optimization. Section 5.4 presents a taxonomy and comparison of various dynamic firewall optimization techniques. Section 5.5 describes the problem of optimizing firewall rule ordering and our proposed heuristic optimization algorithm, implementation, and our evaluation experiments. Finally, Sect. 5.6 concludes our work.

5.2 Background

The main task of packet filters in security policies is to categorize packets based on a set of rules representing the filtering policy. The information used for filtering packets is usually contained in distinct fields in the IPv4 packet header, namely the transport protocol, source IP, source port, destination IP and destination port. Each filtering rule R is an array of field values. A packet p is said to match a rule R if each header-field of p matches the corresponding rule-field of R. In firewalls, each rule R is associated with an action to be performed if a packet matches a rule. These actions indicate whether to block ("deny") or forward ("permit") the packet to a particular interface. For example, a filtering rule $R = (\text{TCP, } 140.192.*:23, *:*, \text{ permit})$ matches the traffic destined only to subnet 140.192 and TCP destination port 23 and allows it to cross the network boundary.

A firewall policy typically consists of an ordered list of n packet filtering rules $R_1, R_2, \ldots, R_n$ such that packets are sequentially matched against these rules until a matching rule is found. If a packet does not match any of the rules in the policy, then it is discarded because the default rule (last rule) is assumed to be deny [5]. The filtering rules may not be disjoint, and thus packets may match one or more rules in the firewall policy [3]. In this case, these rules are said to be *dependent* and their

	protocol	source address : port	destination address : port	action
1	tcp,	*.*.*.*:any,	161.120.33.41:25,	permit
2	tcp,	140.192.37.30:any,	*.*.*.*:21,	deny
3	tcp,	*.*.*.*:any,	161.120.33.*:21,	deny
4	tcp,	140.192.37.*:any,	*.*.*.*:21,	permit
5	tcp,	*.*.*.*:any,	161.120.33.*:22,	permit
6	tcp,	140.192.37.*:any,	*.*.*.*:80,	deny
7	tcp,	*.*.*.*:any,	161.120.33.40:80,	permit
8	tcp,	*.*.*.*:any,	161.120.33.43:53,	permit
9	udp,	*.*.*.*:any,	161.120.33.43:53,	permit

Fig. 5.1 An example of a typical firewall packet filtering policy showing relation between rules 2, 3 and 4, and between rules 5 and 6

relative ordering must be preserved for the firewall policy to operate correctly. For any two dependent rules that have different filtering actions, the rule that must have an earlier order is said to have higher *precedence* relative to the following related rule. The example filtering policy shown in Fig. 5.1 includes relations dependency between rules 2, 3 and 4, and between rules 5 and 6. The *dependency ratio* of a filtering policy is defined as the ratio of rules that depend on subsequent rule(s) other than the default, and the *dependency depth* is the average number of rules involved in the dependency relations. In our example policy, the dependency ratio is $\frac{2+1}{9}$ and the dependency depth is $\frac{3+2}{2}$.

The filtering rules may not be disjoint, thereby packets may match one or more rules in the firewall policy. In this case, these rules are said to be dependent or overlapping and their relative ordering must be preserved for the firewall policy to operate correctly. For example, in Fig. 5.2a, rules R_1 and R_2 are overlapping rules.

The traffic address space is the space whose elements contains all possible tuples that identify traffic flows in a network environment. This is usually composed of the transport protocol, source address/port, and destination address/port. A segment is a subset of the total traffic address space that is covered by a unique set of rules. In other words, segments are equivalence classes over packets. The equivalence of packets is defined by the same policy rules that match these packets. Therefore, segments exhibit the following two properties: (1) all segments are pairwise disjoint, and (2) any packet must fall in exactly one segment. Figure 5.2a shows a simple firewall policy composed of three rules: R_1, R_2, and R_3. Figure 5.2b shows the segmentation of the firewall policy in Fig. 5.2a. As a result of intersecting (or overlapping) the three rules, four address segments are produced: S_1, S_2, S_3, and S_4.

Typically, a firewall matches all incoming and outgoing packets against the rules in the firewall filtering policy in sequential order. Therefore, the amount of packet matching is obviously proportional to the depth of the matching rules. Intuitively,

a	Rule	protocol	source address:port	destination address:port	action
	R_1	tcp	140.192.37.30:any	*.*.*.*:any	deny
	R_2	tcp	140.192.37.*:100	*.*.*.*:any	accept
	R_3	tcp	*.*.*.*:any	*.*.*.*:any	deny

b

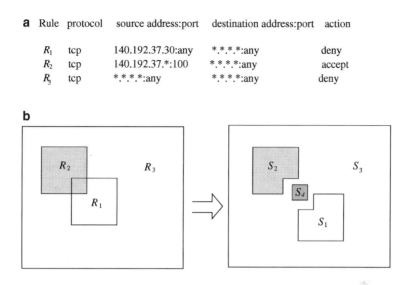

Fig. 5.2 An example of firewall rules and segmentation

this implies that matching can be reduced if rules that match the most significant portion of the traffic are moved to as early order as possible in the filtering policy [6]. The challenge though is on how to dynamically achieve this optimization without introducing rules anomalies as shown in Chap. 1.

5.3 Motivation for Dynamic Firewall Configuration

The behavior of Internet traffic retains several characteristics that can be exploited in the optimization of packet filters. In this section, we highlight some important Internet flow properties that we observed as a result of the traffic analysis that was performed on several Internet packet traces collected at the edge routers of a private academic institution and University of Auckland networks [23]. The traces are stored as 1-h packet header logs at different days of week and times of day, where each log contains the header information for 3–10 M packets that reflect realistic network conditions. After studying the statistics of these traffic traces, we observed the following properties pertaining to Internet flows.

Skewed flow sizes: A flow size is defined as the number of packets that constitute the flow. Referring to Fig. 5.3a, about 20 % of the flows have 10 packets or more, and carry about 70 % of the total traffic. This means that the majority of Internet traffic is constituted by a small number of heavy-weight flows. Therefore, when performing packet filtering, it is desirable to decrease the number of packet matches required for heavy-weight flows in order to reduce the overall packet matching time.

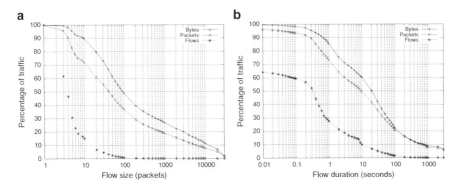

Fig. 5.3 CCDF distribution of (**a**) flow size, and (**b**) flow duration for Internet traces at the University of Auckland

Skewed flow durations: A flow duration is defined as the time elapsed between receiving the first and last packets in the flow. Figure 5.3b, shows that about 20 % of the flows last 5 s or more, and carry about 60 % of the total traffic. This means that the majority of Internet traffic is constituted by a small number of long-lived flows. Therefore, to speed-up the packet filtering process, it is desirable to decrease the number of packet matches required for long-lived flows.

Since all packets of a flow generally match the same filtering rule, our observations clearly indicate that few of the firewall policy rules are actually used for matching a significant portion of the traffic throughout considerable intervals of time. We call this property the *locality of matching* in firewall filtering. Previous studies [8] also support our conclusion as they show that about 90 % of the packets match as little as 25 % of the filtering rules in a large number of ingress routers/firewalls. This emphasizes that the idea of considering the contribution of rule matching in filtering policy optimization is useful and practical for improving the overall matching performance in firewalls.

5.4 Taxonomy of Dynamic Firewall Configuration Techniques

5.4.1 Matching Optimization Techniques

The objective of matching optimization is to reduce the number of rules to be inspected in average case [15]. As shown in Fig. 5.4, there are two types of matching optimization techniques: static and adaptive. Many algorithmic-based techniques have been proposed for static filtering optimization. These techniques try to improve the search time using various algorithmic techniques such as hardware-based solutions, specialized data structures and heuristics. However, these static techniques are used to improve the worst-case scenario and they do not consider the properties of network traffic. The earliest work to exploit traffic properties for packet classification is by Gupta et al. in [13]. In this work, the authors used depth-constrained single-field alphabetic trees to reduce lookup time of destination IP addresses of packets against entries in the routing table. However one cannot directly use it for firewalls which have multiple matching fields. In this chapter, we focus on adaptive optimization techniques that improve the efficiency of filtering in average case. These techniques can adjust the filtering policies to fit the matching frequency of firewall rules or filtering field values. Rule based techniques include *common branch decision tree, offline statistical-based rule generation* and *dynamic rule ordering*. Field value based techniques include *multi-field alphabetic tree, Huffman tree based filtering* and *segment list based filtering*. In the following subsections, we will describe these traffic-aware dynamic firewall policy techniques because they represent the state-of-the-art of traffic-aware firewall filtering for firewalls with large number of overlapping rules.

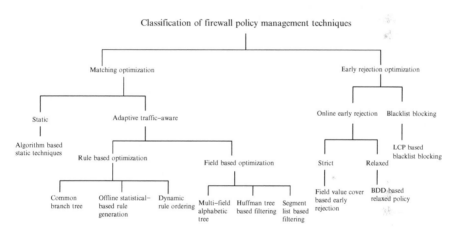

Fig. 5.4 Classification of dynamic firewall configuration techniques

5.4.1.1 Rule Based Optimization

Common Branch Tree: In [8], the authors present common branching tree based packet classification algorithms in an operational network. Decision trees can be categorized under three optimization criteria: worst-case, average case and mixed. Based on the skewness in Internet traffic, they suggest that average-case time is an important metric in the packet classification settings and propose algorithms to construct common branches decision trees to achieve good average-case performance. It needs time $\Theta(klog(l/k))$ and space $\Theta(l)$ to build common branches decision tree, where l is the number of rules and k is the number of fields.

The experimental evaluation on real-word filters showed that common branches trees use much less memory than binary decision trees and have comparable worst-case and average-case search times. The good performance of common branching tree can be attributed to the presence of extensive wildcarding with certain structure in the rule sets. The limitation of the technique is that the entire decision tree needs to be rebuilt every time when the traffic pattern changes, and it is not appropriate for heavily overlapping rules.

Offline Statistical-Based Rule Generation: In [27], the authors presented an offline statistical-based rule generation technique called Traffic-aware Firewall Optimizer (TFO). The first step in TFO is called *Pre-Optimization*. This step will remove all redundancies in the rule set. The second step of TFO uses two optimizers: a *rule set based* optimizer and a *traffic based* optimizer. The rule set based optimizer contains the *Disjoint Set Creator (DSC)* algorithm and the *Disjoint Set Merger (DSM)* algorithm. The DSC algorithm converts the original rule set to a semantically equivalent disjoint rule set, which can provide the traffic based optimizer with full flexibility to re-order rules based on traffic characteristics. The DSM algorithm merges the rules of the disjoint rule set produced by DSC to reduce rule set size. The traffic based optimizer has four components, namely *hot caching, total re-ordering, default proxy*, and *online adaptation*. The hot caching scheme tries to put those rules that are frequently hit to the top of the rule set. The total re-ordering scheme combines the measure of hit frequency and rule size to optimize rule ordering. The default proxy scheme can optimize the firewall performance when the default deny action is heavily invoked. The online adaptation scheme builds long-term rule hit profile to optimize the rule set.

TFO is based on the assumption that only a small portion of rules are dependent on other rules, so it cannot handle policies with heavily overlapped rules. Also, TFO has only limited adaptivity because the rule hit profile is built offline. The authors conducted experiments in only one enterprise firewall, which may not be able to represent other real world firewalls.

Dynamic Rule Ordering: This technique uses a heuristic approximation algorithm for optimal dynamic firewall rule ordering based on real-time traffic characteristics [14]. The objective of optimizing the firewall rules is to create a semantically equivalent rule order that minimizes the packet matching time in firewalls. The Optimal Rule Ordering (ORO) problem is mapped to the job scheduling problem for a single machine with precedence constraints. Since the scheduling problem is NP-hard, the general ORO problem is also NP-hard. Thus a heuristic approximation algorithm that runs in polynomial time and achieves near-optimal results for the most common firewall policies is presented.

The implementation of the technique also includes a method to compute filtering rule weights in order to capture the matching importance of every rule relative to others. Each rule in the filtering policy is given a weight that reflects the dominance of this rule in matching the traffic processed by the firewall. The rule weight is calculated based on *matching frequency*, which determines how frequent the rule has been triggered, and *matching recency*, which determines how recent the rule has been triggered during packet matching. The optimized rule list is constructed based on the computed rule weights and is used for matching upcoming packets to the firewall. Since the traffic distribution of Internet flows over filtering rules is constantly changing, the rule weights should be dynamically adjusted to reflect the most recent distribution. Two types of rule list updates are used: *performance-based triggered* updates and *time-based* periodic updates. In this way, an ordering that is as close as possible to the optimal can be computed, while the overhead to compute these updates can be minimized.

This technique seems to be the most practical proposed technique in this domain as it does not require any translation or adaption of the firewall policy in order to implement dynamic configuration optimization. The limitation of the technique is that it is not work well with policies of a large number of overlapping rules. However, this is usually uncommon in firewall policies.

5.4.2 Field Based Optimization

Multi-field Alphabetic Tree: In [15, 17], a new multi-field alphabetic tree based technique for dynamic firewall policy management was presented. The technique calculates the field value frequency (entropy) and uses this entropy information to build the alphabetic search tree for adaptive packet filtering. The alphabetic search tree stores field values in the leaves based on given weights such that the inherent order of the stored values is preserved. At each internal node, the left subtree contains nodes that have values less than those at the right hand-side. This added constraint of enforcing an order on the placement of values in the tree enables the matching algorithm to branch left or right. The constraint can also eliminate the need for preprocessing of the packet field values. The alphabetic search tree inserts values of higher occurrence probability (matching frequency) at higher tree levels than the values with less probability. Field values that commonly exist in the traffic will have less number of packet matches compared to uncommon values.

The alphabetic search tree can improve the overall average filtering by significantly reducing the number of matches for most popular packets, though it may not be in favor of less-frequently matched traffic. The gain in the filtering performance is proportional to the degree of skewness in the traffic distribution over field values. Even in the worst case scenario when the traffic distribution is uniform, this technique cannot do worse than the binary search as a lower bound.

The alphabetic search tree can be build with time $O(nlogn)$ and space $O(n)$ where n is the number of rules. The limitation of this technique is that the overhead of updating the tree can be significant.

Huffman Tree Based Filtering: This technique in [1] uses Huffman tree to represent the segmentation of traffic address space in the firewall policy. The Huffman tree can minimize the average number of comparisons applied on packets arriving at the firewall ports.

To build the Huffman tree, the traffic statistics can be kept as hit-count measurements for every segments. The internal nodes of the Huffman tree contain a Boolean expression that should be satisfied by each packet passing through this node towards its descendants. The expression is built by taking logic OR of the two corresponding expressions from the children nodes. When a new node is created in a merging step of two nodes with the lowest weight, it will have the expression that takes the logic OR of these two nodes.

The operation in the Huffman tree building algorithm differs slightly with the original Huffman's algorithm. The changes occur in swapping the left and right children based on whichever is easier to evaluate. Another difference is the added expression at each node.

The time and space complexity of building the Huffman tree are $O(ns)$ and s respectively, where n is the number of rules and s is the number of segments in the policy. Using the skewness of the segments to build a Huffman tree over these segments can enhance the performance of searching. The technique is good for policies with a large number of rules. The limitation is that the Huffman tree needs to be rebuilt periodically to reflect the changes in the network flows.

Segment List Based Filtering: In order to get rid of the maintenance cost of the Huffman tree, one can use policy segments-based search list [1] to utilize the very high imbalance in the frequency distribution of packets over the policy segments. One can obtain a very simple yet extremely effective structure by building a simple list of segments that is updated after each packet match. Theoretically, the optimal order is to have the segments sorted in reverse order of their popularity. But it is impossible to guarantee this without prior knowledge of the exact distribution. A heuristic algorithm can be used to minimize the average search time. The main idea in the algorithm is to match an incoming packet against the segment list one-by-one, and once a match is found, the list ordering will be adjusted.

The time and space complexity of to build the segment list are $O(ns)$ and s respectively, where n is the number of rules and s is the number of segments in the policy. This technique only contains very simple operations. It is good for extremely biased traffic. The only limitation is that it has a transient behavior until a good order of segments is obtained.

5.4.3 Early Rejection Optimization Techniques

The problem of early packet filters received much attention for two main reasons. The first is to protect firewalls from DoS attacks that target the default deny rule. The second is to minimize the filtering overhead due to discarding unwanted traffic by introducing approximate policies that can easily filter out discarded traffic.

Early rejection optimization can be classified as *online* and *blacklist blocking*. Online early rejection techniques include *field value cover early rejection* [17] and *BDD based relaxed policy* [2]. Blacklist blocking techniques include *LCP based blacklist blocking* [10].

5.4.3.1 Online Early Rejection

Field Value Cover Based Early Rejection: The first paper to present an early rejection optimization technique is [17]. In this technique, an early filtering module is deployed as another layer before the actual filtering that takes place in a firewall. The goal of this early filtering module is to filter out as many discarded packets as possible with the lowest overhead. This is because discarded packets might traverse a long decision path of rule matching before they are finally rejected by the default deny rule, which causes significant overhead proportional to the number of rules in the firewall policy. For those packets that the early filtering module has made a decision (deny or accept), there is no need to pass the packet to the original filtering module. If the early filtering module cannot reach a decision based on its approximation of the policy, then the filtering process will be delegated to the original filtering algorithm.

The early rejection rules (RR) can be formed as a combination of the common field values that cover all rules in the policy. It can be shown that these rules are more feasible to find because the number of distinct field values is usually small relative to the policy size. It is desirable to search in the firewall policy for a combination of common field values such that every rule uses at least one of these values. This problem can be modeled as a set cover problem. Two approximation algorithms can be used to solve this problem. The first one runs in time $O(n^2)$ and has an approximation ratio $log(n)$ where n is the number of rules. The second one uses integer programming to achieve an f approximation ratio where f is the maximum number of subsets that any element can belong to. The set cover approximation algorithm generates a combination of common field values to be used as early rejection rules. But it is not known in advance how many and which ones that we should use to achieve an optimal rejection solution. A suit of three algorithms were used to address this problem. These three algorithms are the *startup phase algorithm, dynamic rule selection algorithm* and *early rejection algorithm*. In the *startup phase algorithm*, the candidate rejection rule list is built from different solutions that belong to the set cover problem. The *dynamic rule selection algorithm* is responsible for the periodic addition/removal of rules according to the performance gain/loss of each rule. The *early rejection algorithm* calculates the location of early rejection relative to normal packet filtering and defines the per-packet operation of filtering. The limitation of the technique is that it is not suitable for large policies (policies with a large number of rules).

BDD Based Relaxed Policy: Another technique is called BDD (Binary Decision Diagram) based relaxed policy. The basic idea of BDD based relaxed policy is to approximate the current policy with another new policy. The technique evaluates every packet against the new policy, and decide to accept, reject, or forward it to the original policy. The original policy is deployed as normal, but it is not executed unless the early filtering module fails to reach a decision.

Efficient Boolean expression can be used to represent and approximate the policy. The actual implementation is based on Boolean expressions, which are constructed using BDD. Each Boolean expression represents the different packets that match a specific rule, and the variables used for this expression correspond to the bits of individual packet header fields (e.g., source IP, destination port, protocol, etc). BDDs can facilitate the matching by representing the expression in the form of a tree, where each variable is checked only once. An important advantage of the BDD tree is that the decision can be quickly made for a large portion of the packet space. When a packet arrives, the fields in the packet header are extracted and sorted according to their order in the expression tree, so they can be used one-by-one in navigating the tree. Tree navigation is itself a very simple set of instructions. One needs only to check the variable at the current node, load the left child node entry in the BDD table if true and the right child entry if false. This is repeated until a node is reached with a final value or reaching the maximum depth allowed in the tree. Note that this BDD construction technique can also be used for matching optimization.

The whole system is dynamic to traffic properties and can be tuned by the policy structure and previous performance measures. The limitation of the technique is that the overhead to build the BDD is usually significant.

5.4.3.2   LCP Based Blacklist Blocking

This technique is the general framework for modeling the filter selection as resource allocation problems in [10]. A filter is a set of simple access control rules to specify that the addresses with certain prefixes should be blocked. The goal of filter selection is to build filtering rules that can minimize the impact of malicious sources in the network using the available network resources. The technique considers different filtering problems based on different attack scenarios, operators' policies and constraints. Each filtering problem can be modeled as an optimization problem. The data structure to represent the problems is the Longest Common Prefix (LCP) tree. The LCP tree is a kind of binary tree such that the leaves of the tree are the malicious IP addresses and all the other nodes represent the longest common prefixes between any pair of IPs in the tree. The LCP tree can be built in time $O(mN)$ and space $O(N)$ where $m = 32$ is the number of bits in the IP address and N is the number of malicious IP addresses. Polynomial or pseudo-polynomial algorithms were designed to solve the filtering problems. The limitation of this technique is that all the malicious IP addresses must be known before the computation of the optimal solution. To defend the attackers who can move quickly among multiple source IPs, one need to re-compute the optimal solutions frequently. This technique may not be efficient enough in this case.

5.4.4   A Comparative Study

In this section we present a detailed comparison for the traffic-aware dynamic firewall policy management techniques discussed in the chapter.

Table 5.1 shows the comparison for the data structure, algorithm, adaptivity, measurement and complexity (time and space) of the techniques. Here the "adaptivity" column denotes whether the technique is online or offline, and the "measurement" column denotes the key quantitative values used in the technique. We compare the nine techniques discussed in the chapter for traffic-aware packet filtering. The algorithmic-based static techniques in Fig. 5.4 are not included in our study since they are not traffic-aware filtering techniques. Note that in the table, n, d, s, and N are the number of rules, the number of fields, the number of segments, and the number of malicious source addresses in the policy, respectively. For BDD based techniques, in the worst case the complexity can be exponential. However, in most cases, the complexity of BDD construction for firewall policies does not exceed the quadratic of the number of rules due to rule correlation and overlapping [9]. For *offline statistical-based rule generation*, the complexity is not known because the authors did not give a complexity analysis. We can note that *dynamic rule ordering* and *multi-field alphabetic tree* have similar complexity, while *Huffman tree based filtering* and *segment list based filtering* have complexity related to the number of rules and segments in the policy.

Table 5.2 compares the functionality, policy structure, traffic characterization and maintenance cost of each technique. In this table, plus (+) sign means the corresponding technique is suitable for the property, and minus (−) sign means the corresponding technique may not be suitable for the property. N/A means the technique is not applicable for the property. Skewness is the measure of the asymmetry in the probability distribution of the traffic. Dynamic means that the traffic pattern has frequent changes.

LCP based blacklist blocking is not applicable for general policies of multi-field rules. Although *dynamic rule ordering, common branch tree*, and *offline statistical-based rule generation* techniques are good for rules with multiple fields, they are not suitable for heavily overlapping policies. Although *dynamic rule ordering, segment list based filtering, multi-field alphabetic tree* and *Huffman tree based filtering* techniques exhibit high dynamism and low maintenance overhead, they expect high-to-moderate skewness in the traffic distribution (i.e., there is a small number of popular servers) except *dynamic rule ordering*, which can tolerate low skewness in traffic.

BDD based relaxed policy, field value cover based early rejection, and *offline statistical-based rule generation* are not suitable for large policies or policies with large number of field values. *Huffman tree based filtering, common branch tree*, and *offline statistical-based rule generation* could exhibit high maintenance overhead. Online early rejection techniques (*BDD based relaxed policy, field value cover based early rejection*) look robust with traffic distribution and rules overlapping, but they suffer from the high number of rules. It is worth noticing that *Offline statistical-based rule generation* is not fit for overlapping rules and traffic dynamics, and *LCP based blacklist blocking* can only be applied efficiently to a pre-defined blacklist. To achieve the desired goal one should choose the appropriate technique according to the properties of the firewall policy.

Table 5.1 Comparison for the algorithm, data structure and complexity of dynamic firewall configuration techniques

Technique	Structure	Algorithm	Adaptive	Measurement	Time	Space
Common branch tree [8]	Tree	Decision tree	Offline	N/A	$n^{0.63}$	$n^{\Theta(d)}$
Offline statistical-based rule generation [27]	List	Optimal splitting	Offline	N/A	2^n	n
Dynamic rule ordering [14]	Rule	Job scheduling with precedence	Online	Rule frequency and recency	$O(n\log n)$	$O(n)$
Multi-field alphabetic tree [17]	Tree	Alphabetic tree	Online	Field entropy	$O(n\log n)$	$O(dn)$
Huffman tree filtering [1]	Tree	Huffman tree	Online	Segment entropy	$O(ns)$	$O(s)$
Segment list based filtering [1]	List	Linear search	Online	Segment counting	$O(ns)$	$O(s)$
Field value cover based early rejection [17]	Boolean	Set cover approximation	Online	Statistical thresholding	$O(n^2)$	$O(n)$
BDD based relaxed policy [2]	BDD	BDD optimization	Online	Rule probability	$O(2^n)$	$O(2^n)$
LCP based blacklist blocking [10]	Tree	Dynamic programming	Offline	N/A	$O(N)$	$O(N)$

Table 5.2 Comparison for limitation and application suitability of the dynamic firewall configuration techniques (FVs: field values; seg: segments; mod: moderate)

Technique	Functionality		Policy structure					Traffic		
	Match opt	Early rejection	Multi-field	High overlapping	Large policy	Large no. of FVs	Large no. of segs	Skewness	Dynamic	Cost
Common branch tree	+	−	+	−	+	−	N/A	Mod	No	High
Offline statistical-based rule generation	+	+	+	−	−	−	N/A	High	Low	High
Dynamic rule ordering	+	−	+	−	+	+	N/A	Low	High	Low
Multi-field alphabetic tree	+	−	+	+	+	−	N/A	Mode	High	Low
Huffman tree filtering	+	−	+	+	+	N/A	−	Mod	High	Low
Segment list based filtering	+	−	+	+	+	N/A	−	Mod	High	Low
Field value cover based early rejection	−	+	+	+	−	−	N/A	Mod	High	Mod
BDD based relaxed policy	+	+	+	+	−	−	−	Low	Mod	High
LCP based blacklist blocking	−	+	−	−	+	+	N/A	N/A	High	Mod

5.5   Dynamic Firewall Rule Ordering (DRO)

In this section, we study the problem of optimizing the ordering of packet filtering rules to increase the performance of packet matching in firewalls. We show that the general problem is hard to solve in polynomial time, and we present a heuristic approximation algorithm that runs in polynomial time and achieves near-optimal results for the most common firewall policies.

5.5.1   Optimal Rule Ordering Problem

Given a set of filtering rules with inter-rule dependencies and packet matching weights, the optimal rule ordering problem (ORO) is to find a *legitimate* rule ordering that obtains the minimum number of packet matches. The rule ordering solution is legitimate only if the precedence relations between policy rules are preserved. Assuming that packets are sequentially matched against a policy consisting of n filtering rules with d_i as the order (depth) of rule R_i in the policy and w_i is a given weight that resembles the dominance of R_i in packet matching, we can then formally define ORO by the following the minimization problem:

$$\min \sum_{i=1}^{n} w_i d_i \tag{5.1}$$

In order to solve the ORO problem, it can be formalized as an binary integer program (BIP) as follows.

$$\min \sum_{i=1}^{n} \sum_{k=1}^{n} k w_i x_{ik} \tag{5.2}$$

$$\text{subject to } \forall i \sum_{k=1}^{n} x_{ik} = 1 \tag{5.3}$$

$$\forall k \sum_{i=1}^{n} x_{ik} = 1 \tag{5.4}$$

$$\sum_{k=1}^{n} k x_{ik} - \sum_{k=1}^{n} k x_{jk} < 0 \text{ if } R_i \rightarrow R_j \tag{5.5}$$

$$x_{ik} \in \{0,1\}, i \in \{1,\dots,n\}, k \in \{1,\dots,n\}$$

where x_{ik} is a binary variable such that $x_{ik} = 1$ if rule R_i is positioned at location k in the policy, and $x_{ik} = 0$ otherwise. The minimization objective function (5.2) resembles the optimization problem described in 1 where the depth d_i of rule R_i is given by the expression $\sum_{k=1}^{n} k x_{ik}$ and w_i is the rule weight. The computation of rule weights is described later is Sect. 5.5.3.1. Constraint (5.3) guarantees that every rule is positioned at exactly one location, while Constraint (5.4) ensures that any specific location is occupied by exactly one rule. Constraint (5.5) preserves the ordering precedence between dependent rules by ensuring that if rule R_i has higher precedence over rule R_j ($R_i \rightarrow R_j$), then the order of R_i in the policy should come before that of R_j.

The above BIP formalization allows for the use of iterative numeric techniques to solve the ORO problem [4]. A lower bound for the ORO problem can be obtained by relaxing the binary variables into linear variables and solving the BIP equations as a linear programming problem. To obtain an optimal solution, we can apply the branch-and-bound algorithm combined with gradient projection method to reduce the effect of combinatorial explosion. However, a more efficient method is needed to compute the solution since the branch-and-bound method cannot guarantee a computation time that is polynomial in the number of rules [4]. In the following section, we present our approximate heuristic solution for the ORO problem that can achieve a near-optimal solution in polynomial time.

The optimal rule ordering can be achieved when the filtering rules are disjoint by simply sorting the rules in non-increasing order based on their weights [24]. However, typical firewall policies contain dependent rules and therefore simple sorting cannot be used because ordering the rules based on their weights might conflict with rule dependencies. The ORO problem can be mapped to a single machine job scheduling problem with precedence constraints [11, 21]. The job scheduling problem is represented by the notation $\alpha|\beta|\gamma|\delta$, where α is the number of machines, β is the job precedence, γ is processing time restrictions, and δ is the optimization objective function. The ORO problem is similar to the $1|\beta|1|\sum_{i=1}^{n} w_i C_i$ scheduling problem, where w_i is the weight associated with a job and C_i is the job completion time. Since the scheduling problem was proven to be NP-Complete [20], we can prove that the ORO problem is also NP-Complete.

Theorem 5.1. *The optimal firewall rule ordering (ORO) problem is NP-Complete.*

Proof. First, we show that ORO is in NP, i.e., verifiable in polynomial time. Second, we show that ORO is NP-hard by transforming the job scheduling problem $1|\beta|1|\sum_{i=1}^{n} w_i C_i$ to ORO in polynomial time. The transformation is performed by simply mapping jobs with precedence constraints to filtering rules with ordering precedence, and the job completion time C_i to the rule order d_i. Hence, ORO has a solution only if the job scheduling problem also has a solution. Since $1|\beta|1|\sum_{i=1}^{n} w_i C_i$ is NP-Complete, the ORO problem is also NP-Complete. The details of the proof are presented in [16].

5.5.2 Heuristic ORO Algorithm

Although several approximation algorithms have been proposed to solve the $1|\beta|1|\sum_{i=1}^{n} w_i C_i$ problem [25], the best approximation produces a solution $\left(2 - \frac{2}{n+1}\right)$ of the optimal solution, where n is the number of jobs/rules. For a reasonably large number of rules (100–1000 rules), this solution is twice as large as

---

Algorithm 10 OptimizeActiveRules(*rule_list*, *opt_limit*)

1: *weight* ← 0
2: H ← BuildMaxHeap(H, *rule_list*)
3: **while** H is not empty **do**
4:      R_b ← HeapExtractMax(H)
5:      **for all** R_d ∈ {rules dependent on R_b} **do**
6:          **if** R_d ∉ *active_rules* **then**
7:              *current* ← ListTail(*active_rules*)
8:              **while** *current* ≠ nil **do**
9:                  R_a ← ListGet(*current*)
10:                 **if** Weight(R_a) < Weight(R_d) and R_a not depending on R_d **then**
11:                     *current* ← ListPrevious(*current*)
12:                 **else**
13:                     break
14:                 **end if**
15:             **end while**
16:             ListInsertAfter(*current*, R_d)
17:             *weight* ← *weight* + Weight(R_d)
18:             HeapRemove(H, R_d)
19:             ListRemove(*rule_list*, R_d)
20:         **end if**
21:     **end for**
22:     ListInsertTail(*active_rules*, R_b)
23:     ListRemove(*rule_list*, R_b)
24:     **if** *weight* ≥ *opt_limit* **then**
25:         break
26:     **end if**
27: **end while**
28: **for all** R_m ∈ *rule_list* **do**
29:     ListInsertTail(*active_rules*, R_m)
30: **end for**
31: **return** *active_rules*

---

the optimal solution. Moreover, many of the job scheduling approximations rely on transforming the problem and solving it as a linear program, which is a significantly a complex and computationally intensive process for practical firewall deployment.

For these reasons, we developed a new heuristic approximation algorithm for the ORO problem that is more efficient and practical to implement in firewalls. The algorithm considers three common properties in real firewall filtering rules: (1) the distribution of rule weights is highly skewed such that a few number of rules match the majority of the Internet traffic, (2) the dependency depth of rule relations is limited to a few number of rules, and (3) the number of dependent rules is small relative to the total number of rules in the firewall policy.

Algorithm 10 describes the details of our heuristic. The algorithm takes as an input the rule list to be optimized and an *optimization limit* that represents an upper bound on the total weight of the selected rules in the optimization process, these are called the *active rules*. It first creates a Max-Heap [18] of filtering rules based on their weights (Line 2). The Max-Heap data structure stores the item with the maximum weight on the top, such that it can be retrieved in constant time. Rules (also called *base rules*) are sequentially picked from the heap in descending order according to their weights (Line 4). With every base rule removed from the heap, all dependent rules that must precede this rule are also removed from the heap and then inserted in the correct order in the optimized active rule list (Lines 6–17). Each dependent rule is inserted in the active rule list such that the rules in the list are in descending order according to their weights (Lines 8–12), then, the base rule is appended to the optimized list (Lines 10–11). This procedure is repeated until the total of all rules weights in the optimized list exceeds the weight optimization limit (Lines 22–24). Finally, all the remaining rules in the original list are appended to the optimized active list according to their original order (Lines 26–28).

The time complexity of the algorithm is determined by the two cascaded loops and the heapification operation, however, heapification is performed in $O(n \lg n)$ and can be ignored. Therefore, theoretically, the algorithm optimizes a list of n rules in $O(n^2)$ running time. However, the actual running time is only a fraction of this upper bound since every time a base rule is picked from the heap, all its dependent rules are also removed. This results in rapidly decreasing the total number of iterations in the outer while loop (Lines 3–25), and reducing the heapification time (Line 4) as well. In addition, using the optimization weight limit significantly reduces the number of iterations in the inner while loop (Lines 8–15) by considering only the most active rules. Our study in Sect. 5.5.4 indicates that it is sufficient to optimize the most active 25–45 % of the rules in the policy. The space complexity is obviously bounded by $O(n)$ since the algorithm keeps only two lists of filtering rules.

Notice that our algorithm uses a doubly-linked list implementation of the rule lists in order to reduce the time needed for rule insertion. Also notice that the set of rules preceding each rule in the policy can be easily accessed through a linked list of pointers created in a policy pre-processing phase [16]. This pre-processing is performed only when the firewall is bootstrapped or when the filtering policy is modified.

5.5.3 Implementation of Dynamic Rule Ordering

In this section, we describe the implementation details of our rule order optimization mechanism in real firewalls. The implementation includes a method to compute filtering rule weights in order to capture the matching importance of every rule relative to other rules in the policy, and an adaptation mechanism that triggers the optimization algorithm only when needed based on the most recent traffic conditions.

5.5.3.1 Computation of Rule Weights

Each rule in the filtering policy is given a weight that reflects the matching dominance of this rule relative to other rules in the policy. The rule weight calculation should consider two main factors: (1) *matching frequency*, which determines how frequent the rule has been triggered, and (2) *matching recency*, which determines how recent the rule has been triggered in the packet matching process. Rule frequency and recency are significantly important as they indicate how likely the rule will match a packet in the future as a result of the locality of matching property. Based on this property, rules with higher matching frequency and that has been recently triggered are more likely to get triggered by the next filtered packet.

To estimate the weight of a rule, we begin by calculating the matching frequency of this rule. The frequency factor ϕ_i of rule R_i in any time interval can be expressed as the ratio of number of packets p_i matching this rule to the total number of packets P matched by the firewall in the same interval.

$$\phi_i = \frac{p_i}{P} \quad \text{where} P = \sum_{i=1}^{n} p_i \tag{5.6}$$

Equation (5.6) captures the matching frequency of a rule relative to other rules in the policy during a given interval of time. However, it cannot express the matching recency of this rule in the policy since it does not distinguish between rules that were triggered at the beginning and others triggered at the end of the same time interval. As discussed later in Sect. 5.5.3.2, rule weights are calculated only when rule ordering updates are needed. Therefore, for relatively long intervals between consecutive rule order updates (update intervals), rules that have not been triggered for a relatively long duration should be given less weight than other rules that are currently actively matching packets. This can be achieved by scaling the matching frequency of each rule using a recency factor ρ_i that captures the matching recency of the rule. Thus, the effective rule weight w_i of rule R_i can be given by the formula:

$$w_i = \rho_i \phi_i \tag{5.7}$$

To capture the matching recency of a rule, we define the *rule idle time* t_i as the interval of time elapsed since a packet has lastly triggered rule R_i during the current update interval. Using the rule idle time, we propose two different approaches to compute the rule recency factor using statistical and deterministic computations as follows.

Statistical computation of rule recency: A statistical approach is used to keep track of the time gaps in-between packets matched by the same rule in order to compute how likely a packet will hit this rule after a given idle time. We assume that we have a finite number m of possible inter-packet time gap values T_k for all rules in the policy such that $0 < T_k < T_{k+1}$. The *packet gap probability* $P(p|T_k)$ estimates how likely a packet p will match a certain rule after a packet gap T_k, which can be expressed using Bayesian probability [22] as follows:

$$P(p|T_k) = P(p) \frac{P(T_k|p)}{P(T_k)} \tag{5.8}$$

where $P(p)$ is the packet matching probability of the rule computed using Eq. (5.6). $P(T_k|p)$ is the probability that T_k appears for this rule, which is equal to the ratio of packets preceded by T_k to the total number of packets matching the rule. $P(T_k)$ is the probability of occurrence of packet gap T_k in the entire policy and can be computed as the ratio of the total number of packets preceded by T_k in all rules, to the total number of packets processed by the policy. Thus, at any instant of time, the recency factor of rule R_i is given as:

$$\rho_i = P(p|T_k) \quad \text{such that } T_{k-1} < t_i < T_{k+1} \tag{5.9}$$

The number of packet gap intervals and the size of each gap should be determined based on the traffic statistics collected by the firewall. A simple approach to set these intervals is to use the maximum (T_{max}) and minimum (T_{min}) packet gap values seen by the firewall so far to build a Fibonacci number series as follows:

$$T_1 = T_2 = T_{min}, \quad T_k = T_{k-1} + T_{k-2}, \quad T_m \le 2T_{max}, \quad 1 < k \le m \tag{5.10}$$

In order to get the occurrence probability of different packet gap values, the firewall should maintain a data structure for every rule to record the number of matching packets preceded by such gaps. The data structure stores packet counters sorted in an ascending order based on their corresponding gap values to speed up the lookup operation needed in Eq. (5.9).

Deterministic computation of rule recency: Although the statistical approach provides an accurate estimation of rule recency, it involves computationally intensive operations that may impact the performance of low-end filtering devices with limited processing power. Therefore, we propose an alternative light-weight deterministic approach to compute rule recency with acceptable accuracy. In this approach, the recency factor of rule R_i is computed using a natural exponential decay function controlled by the ratio of the rule idle time t_i to the average idle time τ for all rules, and a constant *decay factor* β. This can be formulated as follows:

$$\rho_i = e^{-\beta \frac{t_i}{\tau}} \quad \text{where} \quad \beta \ge 0 \tag{5.11}$$

This formula ensures that when the idle time is much larger than average, the rule recency significantly decreases, and vice versa. The decay rate is controlled by β such that if $\beta < 1$, the rule recency slowly decreases as the idle time increases, while when $\beta > 1$, the recency sharply decreases to a zero value. Our evaluation experiments presented in Sect. 5.5.4 show that the best reduction in matching can be achieved with $0.5 \le \beta \le 1$. Based on Eq. (5.11), the longer the rule idle time gets, the less the rule recency becomes, giving a significant advantage for rules that have been triggered towards the end of the update interval.

In order to avoid computationally intensive power calculations in our implementation, we use an approximate linearized version of Eq. (5.11) as follows:

$$\rho_i = \begin{cases} (1 - \beta \frac{t_i}{\tau}) & \text{when } t_i < \frac{\tau}{\beta} \\ 0 & \text{otherwise} \end{cases} \tag{5.12}$$

Notice that in this formula, the rule recency is also controlled by the same factors controlling Eq. (5.11) but with much less computational complexity. Substituting from Eqs. (5.6) and (5.12) in (5.7), the overall weight of rule R_i is computed as follows:

$$w_i = \begin{cases} \frac{p_i}{P}(1 - \beta\frac{t_i}{\tau}) & \text{when } t_i < \frac{\tau}{\beta} \\ 0 & \text{otherwise} \end{cases} \qquad (5.13)$$

Equation (5.13) approximately estimates the weight of a rule relative to other rules in the policy such that, as the idle time for a rule decreases, it's relative weight increases, and vice versa. Thus, less idle rules are given more importance and hence an earlier position in the filtering policy resulting in overall packet matching reduction. Our evaluation study in Sect. 5.5.4 shows that the matching reduction is more sensitive to rule recency in the case of long-lived bursty flows, while it is more sensitive to rule frequency for heavy-weight bulky flows.

Since the rule frequency and recency expressions still include computationally intensive floating point division operations, we need to further simplify the compu-tations in order to calculate the rule weights more efficiently. Instead of using real time as a reference, we use a packet-based virtual clock [31] approach to measure the rule idle time. Simply, the number of packets received so far by the firewall since the last rule order update is used to indicate the virtual time. When a rule matches a packet, the rule packet frequency p_i is incremented, and the current value of the global packet counter P is recorded in a rule register P_i. Replacing the time quantities in Eq. (5.13) with the corresponding packet counters yields:

$$w_i = \begin{cases} \frac{p_i}{P}(1 - \beta\frac{P-P_i}{\tau_p}) = \frac{\beta}{\tau_p P}[p_i(P_i - P + \frac{\tau_p}{\beta})] & \text{when } P_i > P - \frac{\tau_p}{\beta} \\ 0 & \text{otherwise} \end{cases} \qquad (5.14)$$

where $P - P_i$ indicates the virtual rule idle time measured in number packets that have been processed since the rule was lastly triggered, and τ_p is the average virtual idle virtual time of all rules. Thus, for any elapsed interval of time, the *scaled weight* $\tilde{w}_i$ of rule R_i can be calculated as follows:

$$\tilde{w}_i = \frac{\tau_p P}{\beta} w_i = \begin{cases} p_i(P_i - P + \frac{\tau_p}{\beta}) & \text{when } P_i > P - \frac{\tau_p}{\beta} \\ 0 & \text{otherwise} \end{cases} \qquad (5.15)$$

Notice that, with the choice of $\beta = 1$ in Eq. (5.15), the computation of $\tilde{w}_i$ involves only integral arithmetic operations, yet still measures the importance of rule R_i with respect to other rules in the policy. Therefore, $\tilde{w}_i$ can be directly used to represent rule weights in Algorithm 10 with much less processing overhead. Also notice that the weight optimization limit (*opt_limit*) in the algorithm must be multiplied by the scaling factor $\frac{\tau_p P}{\beta}$ for correct comparison with the accumulated scaled weight of the active rules.

Algorithm 11 MatchPacket(p)

1: $packet\_count \leftarrow packet\_count + 1$
2: $time \leftarrow$ GetCurrentTime()
3: $H \leftarrow$ GetPacketHeader(p)
4: $rule \leftarrow$ MatchRule(H, $rule\_list$)
5: **if** $rule \neq$ nil **then**
6:      $action \leftarrow rule.action$
7:      $rule.p_{count} \leftarrow rule.p_{count} + 1$
8:      $rule.p_{register} \leftarrow packet\_count$
9: **else**
10:     $action \leftarrow$ DEFAULT_ACTION
11: **end if**
12: **if** $action =$ ALLOW **then**
13:     ForwardPacket(p)
14: **else**
15:     DiscardPacket(p)
16: **end if**
17: $\bar{h} \leftarrow (1 - \omega) \times \bar{h} + \omega \times rule.order$
18: $\varepsilon \leftarrow K \times \bar{h} - 1$
19: **if** $\varepsilon > \varepsilon_{thr}$
    or $(time - last\_update) >$ UPD_PERIOD **then**
20:     CalculateRuleWeights($rule\_list$)
21:     OptimizeActiveRules($rule\_list$, OPT_THR)
22:     **for all** $rule \in rule\_list$ **do**
23:         $rule.p_{count} \leftarrow 0$
24:         $rule.p_{register} \leftarrow 0$
25:     **end for**
26:     $packet\_count \leftarrow 0$
27:     $last\_update \leftarrow time$
28: **end if**

5.5.3.2 Integration with Packet Matching

The optimized rule list is constructed based on the packet matching history, and is used for matching future upcoming packets to the firewall. Therefore, The reduction in matching is maximal when the upcoming traffic distribution over filtering rules exactly matches the distribution when the list has been constructed. However, since the traffic distribution of Internet flows over filtering rules is constantly changing, the rule weights must be dynamically adjusted to reflect the most recent distribution. Therefore, we propose two types of rule list updates: performance-based triggered updates and time-based periodic updates. Our goal is to dynamically adjust the rule weights to yield an ordering as close as possible to the optimal, while minimizing these updates in order to avoid the associated processing overhead.

Performance-based triggered updates: Optimizing the rule list is computationally intensive and should be performed only when crucially needed. Thus, performance-based updates are only initiated when the observed packet matching performance significantly deviates from the expected optimal matching. We use the *performance deviation factor* ε to measure how far the actual average number of matches deviates from the optimal average number of matches calculated in the last rule list update. We also define the *update interval* as the time elapsed between two consecutive rule list update events. Thus, ε is given using the following formula:

$$\varepsilon = \frac{\sum_{i=1}^{n} p_i d_i}{\sum_{i=1}^{n} q_i d_i} - 1 \tag{5.16}$$

where d_i is the depth of rule R_i, p_i and q_i are the ratios of packets matching R_i in the current and preceding update intervals, respectively.

Although this formula accurately tracks the deviation from optimal matching, it is very expensive to compute at runtime for every packet received by the firewall. Therefore, we calculate the average number of packet matches so far using an exponential moving average $\bar{h}$ as follows:

$$\bar{h}_j = (1 - \omega)\bar{h}_{j-1} + \omega h_j \tag{5.17}$$

where h_j is the depth of the filtering rule that matched packet j. Therefore, the performance deviation can be computed at any instance of time using $\bar{h}$ from the above equation as follows:

$$\varepsilon = \frac{\bar{h}}{\sum_{i=1}^{n} q_i d_i} - 1 = K\bar{h} - 1 \tag{5.18}$$

where $K = 1/\sum_{i=1}^{n} q_i d_i$ is a constant calculated once every time the rule list is optimized. The deviation factor is computed periodically during the packet matching process, and if its value exceeds a certain *deviation threshold*, a new optimized rule list is constructed. The deviation threshold ε_{thr} is a user configurable parameter to specify the maximum acceptable deviation from the optimal average matching.

Time-based periodic updates: Performance-based triggered updates are important to boost the packet matching performance when it significantly drops below the deviation threshold. However, these updates are not sufficient to detect large performance deviation that is just below the threshold even if it lasts for a prolonged time interval. Thus, regardless of the performance deviation, periodic updates are performed at fixed time intervals that are relatively long. Using the latest traffic statistics, a new active rule list is periodically constructed using fresh rule weights in order to boost up the matching performance close to its optimum level. The update period should be configured based on the computational capacity of the filtering device such that these updates consume little processing power.

Packet matching algorithm: Algorithm 11 describes the integration of the adaptive rule order optimization in a typical firewall packet matching module. The algorithm performs the standard packet matching procedure by matching the packet header against the rule list and performing the corresponding filtering action (Lines 2–15). As packets are received, the global packet counter is incremented, the local packet counter and virtual time register of the triggered rule are updated (Lines 1, 6, 7), and the current average number of matches and the performance deviation are computed using Eqs. (5.17) and (5.18) (Line 17). If the current deviation exceeds the allowable threshold or the last periodic update interval expires, the rule order optimization algorithm in invoked after calculating the new rule weights (Lines 19, 21). Then, the global packet counter as well as the counter/register of every rule are reset to zero (Lines 22–26).

It is important to notice that the extra processing added to the packet matching algorithm imposes minor processing overhead. On one hand, the processing of every packet involves only six arithmetic operations (four assignment operations in Lines 1, 2, 7, 8, and two simple addition and multiplication operations in Lines 17, 18). On the other hand, triggered and periodic updates are performed infrequently when rule list update is required as shown in the results of the experiments presented in Sect. 5.5.4.

5.5.4 Performance Evaluation

To study the performance gain of our proposed rule order optimization technique in firewall filtering, we conducted a large set of simulation and packet trace analysis experiments. The gain in performance is measured in terms of the average reduction in the number of packet header comparisons against the policy rules when using our adaptive rule optimization mechanism as compared to linear packet matching using the original unoptimized rule list.

5.5.4.1 Accuracy of Heuristic ORO Algorithm

In this section, we study the accuracy of our heuristic solution for solving the optimal rule ordering problem with different filtering policy characteristics. We conducted a number of simulation experiments to compare our heuristic to the optimal solution produced by solving the BIP model of the ORO problem presented in Sect. 5.5 using MatLab.

In the first experiment, we study the accuracy of our heuristic algorithm in optimizing varying numbers of filtering rules. In these scenarios, all rules are included in the active rule list (optimization limit 100 %), 20 % of the rules are dependent on other rules, and each rule is related to an average of three preceding rules, which resembles common configurations of firewall policies [28]. Rule weights are assigned based on a Zipf distribution [32] of skewness factor 1.2 to reflect the skewed characteristics seen in real Internet traffic [29]. Figure 5.5a shows that the reduction in matching produced by our proposed heuristic is very close to the optimal solution for rule list sizes ranging from 10 to 200 rules. Figure 5.5b shows that the deviation of our technique from the optimal solution is less than 10 %.

The second set of experiments study the impact of the number of active rules included in the optimization on the accuracy of our solution. The set of active rules is chosen from a policy composed of 200 filtering rules with 20 % dependency

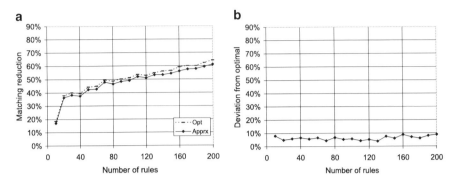

Fig. 5.5 The effect of the total number of rules in the policy on rule order optimization: (**a**) average packet matching reduction; (**b**) deviation from optimal solution

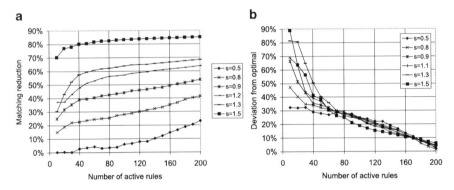

Fig. 5.6 The effect of the number of active rules in the policy on rule order optimization: (**a**) average packet matching reduction; (**b**) deviation from optimal solution

ratio and 3 average dependency depth. The experiment is repeated for different values of the skewness factor s used to calculate the rule weights based on Zipf distribution. Figure 5.6a shows that for all values of s, the reduction in matching increases rapidly as the number of active rules increases up to 25 % of the total number of rules. The experiment results also indicate that increasing the number of active rules beyond this point produces much less improvement, and the rate of improvement is significantly impacted by the skewness of the Zipf distribution. For example, for high skewness values (1.0–1.5), the matching reduction improves only by 10 % when all the rules are included in the optimization. This indicates that even for a large number of firewall rules, optimizing as little as 25 % of the rules is good enough to produce significant improvement in packet matching performance. Figure 5.6b shows that including 25 % of the rules produces a solution within 30 % from optimal. However, more than 80 % of the rules should be optimized in order to get a solution within 10 % from optimal.

We also evaluate how our proposed heuristic performs under various filtering policy configuration styles [30]. Figure 5.7 shows the performance when the average

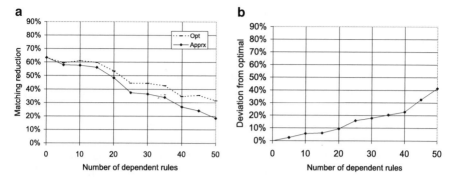

Fig. 5.7 The effect of the average number of dependent rules on rule order optimization: (**a**) average packet matching reduction; (**b**) deviation from optimal solution

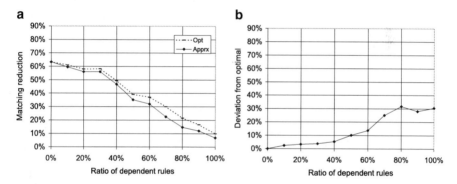

Fig. 5.8 The effect of the average ratio of dependent rules on rule order optimization: (**a**) average packet matching reduction; (**b**) deviation from optimal solution

number of dependent rules varies from a few up to 50 rules. We notice that, as the number of dependent rules significantly increases, the matching reduction decreases in both the optimal as well as heuristic ordering. This is because increasing the number of rules in the dependency relation limits the possibility of finding more rule ordering solutions and thus imposes more constraints on the optimization results. This figure also shows that our heuristic gives results very close to the optimal solution when a relatively small number of dependent rules exists. For 10 or less dependent rules, our heuristics is within 5–10 % from the optimal solution. As the number of dependent rules increases, the deviation from optimal significantly increases. Figure 5.8 shows the performance as the ratio of dependent rules in the policy increases. Even for moderate dependency ratio values (less than 40 %), our heuristic solution is as close as 5–10 % from optimal. In conclusion, our proposed algorithm achieves near optimal results in practical cases where firewall configurations contain less than 40 % dependent rules with 10 rules or less in a dependency relation.

5.5.4.2 Simulation and Traffic Trace Experiments

In this section, we investigate the parameter tuning for our mechanism in order to achieve the best performance under different traffic conditions. For this purpose, we conducted many experiments using simulated as well as real Internet traffic traces. The traffic simulation experiments are conducted using the SimJava discrete event simulator [26], and the firewall packet filtering including rule order optimization is implemented in Java. Different variations of bursty and bulky traffic blends are generated with inter-packet time gaps following exponential distributions [29], and the packet headers are generated such that the matching distribution among the filtering rules follows a dynamically changing Zipf distribution. In addition, we used our firewall simulator to evaluate the optimization performance of our solution using a wide variety of Internet packet traces [23]. The traffic traces are collected from a client-oriented network were the majority of outbound and inbound traffic is composed of requests and responses between local users and public Internet servers, respectively. The outbound traffic is mostly bursty as it is composed of small payloads of service requests, while the inbound traffic is mostly bulky since it carries large response payloads. Based on the traffic flow information in the traces, we generated filtering rules to handle inbound and outbound traffic such that these rules are created to match the IP header field values in these flows. The size of the generated policy (200 rules) typically resembles a reasonable rule list size in real firewall policies [30].

Effect of recency factor: In this experiment, we study the effect of the recency factor on matching performance using both statistical (probabilistic) and deterministic (exponential) estimation of rule recency. Figure 5.9a presents the results of the simulation experiment for different traffic mixes. The graph shows a significant gain in matching reduction when the rule recency factor is applied. The improvement in matching reduction using exponential recency reaches up to 12 % for mostly bursty traffic, while probabilistic recency can achieve a higher gain of 16 %. The figure also shows that probabilistic recency produces better performance gain than the exponential method especially for mostly bulky traffic because of its persistent nature that helps in producing accurate rule weight statistics. However, with mostly bursty traffic, the improvement is marginal, which may not justify for the large processing overhead involved in this method especially with filtering devices of limited processing capacity. Figure 5.9b shows similar results for real Internet traffic traces where the outbound matching reduction is improved by about 20 % with a very small difference between the probabilistic and exponential methods.

The results of another experiment to understand the effect of exponential rule recency are shown in Fig. 5.10a, b for both simulated and real traffic, respectively. The graphs show that, as the decay factor (β) increases up to a value of 1, bursty flows exhibit increasing performance gain whereas bulky flows exhibit slight gains. This can be intuitively explained by the fact that traffic bursts are not likely to coexist in all active rules at exactly the same time, which means that only a few active rules are actually matching packets at any instant of time. This behavior is exploited by the recency factor that gives the opportunity for the actively matching rules to be

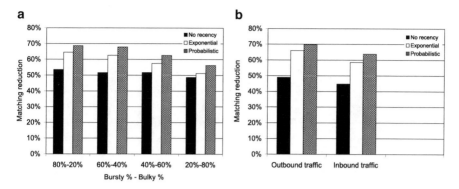

Fig. 5.9 The effect of rule recency factor on average matching reduction when packet filtering is applied to (**a**) simulated traffic; (**b**) real Internet traffic

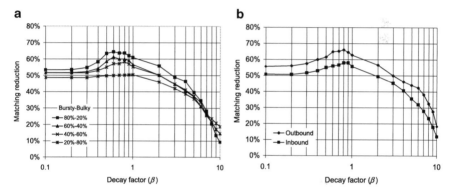

Fig. 5.10 The effect of the recency decay factor on average matching reduction when packet filtering is applied to (**a**) simulated traffic; (**b**) real Internet traffic

pushed ahead of less active ones resulting in less packet matching. Thus, the rule recency is more sensitive to traffic bursts that last for short time intervals, while on the other hand it tends to ignore bulky traffic lasting for relatively longer intervals. When the decay factor is increased beyond 1, the matching reduction decreases dramatically due to the fact that Eq. (15) reduces most of the rule weights to zero, which diminishes the effectiveness of the rule ordering algorithm.

The recency ratio can be chosen based on the nature of the traffic flowing in the filtering device. Our experiments indicate that when bursty flows are dominant, a decay factor of 0.5–1.0 could be used, while it should be within 0.8–1.0 for dominant bulky flows. The traffic characteristics can be easily measured using widely available traffic measuring equipment like Netflow [7], and the corresponding recency ratio values can be retrieved from lookup tables constructed using simulated traffic. From our experiment, we observed that a 1.0 decay factor achieves matching gain close to the best possible results for both bursty and bulky flows.

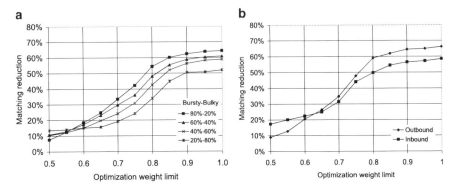

Fig. 5.11 The effect of optimization weight limit on average matching reduction when packet filtering is applied to (**a**) simulated traffic; (**b**) real Internet traffic

Effect of optimization weight limit: In this experiment, we study the effect of the optimization weight limit on packet matching performance. The simulation experiment results shown in Fig. 5.11a indicate that for bursty flows, the matching reduction increases rapidly with increasing the optimization weight up to a plateau value where the matching reduction is almost constant. The matching reduction reaches its highest value when the aggregate active rule weights reach 90 % of the total rule weights, and the active rule list includes about 45 % of the rules in the policy. The results of the same experiment carried on Internet traffic traces are shown in Fig. 5.11b. The graph reflects similar results, with a matching reduction plateau at a weight limit of 80 % corresponding to about 25 % of the rules. These results show that using an optimization weight limit of about 80–90 % significantly reduces the number of rules included in the active list optimization.

Tuning of triggered updates: In this experiment, we closely examine the dynamics of the adaptive rule list update mechanism against real Internet packet traces collected during a 1 h interval on a weekday from 12:00 p.m. to 12:59 p.m. The performance deviation is calculated periodically every 10 s based on the formulas in Sect. 5.5.3.2 and sampled every 100 s for plotting purposes. Meanwhile, the active rule list is dynamically reconstructed whenever the average number of matches deviates significantly from the optimal value. Figure 5.12a shows the results of this experiment with rule list updates indicated by the solid triangular marks.

The graph shows that the performance deviation changes smoothly with every packet received, thus ignoring sudden short-term decrease in the instantaneous matching performance. When the matching performance trend sustains a continuous decline, the deviation factor exceeds the designated threshold and the optimized list is reconstructed based on the most recent rule weights. The frequency of rule list updates is tightly coupled with the deviation threshold ε_{thr} and the averaging smoothing factor ω. Our study of various settings of these parameters show that,

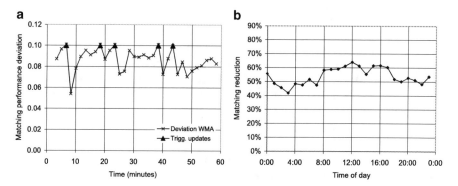

Fig. 5.12 Dynamics of rule order optimization: (**a**) deviation from optimal performance during a rush hour. (**b**) Hourly-average matching reduction throughout a weekday

during rush hours, our adaptive technique reconstructs the list only 2–5 times in an hour when $\omega = 0.4$ and $\varepsilon_{thr} = 0.1$. This incurs minor amortized overhead throughout the full interval in which the optimization algorithm is utilized.

Long-term optimization performance: Figure 5.12b shows the performance of our technique with real Internet traffic traces for an extended period of time starting from 12:00 a.m. to 11:59 p.m. on a weekday. It is clear from this figure that the relative matching gain does not persist at a specific level for a long period of time. The maximum gain (around 60 %) is achieved during day hours where fast filtering is highly needed, and can be attributed to the existence of a large traffic volume that consequently creates significant skewness in the rule matching statistics. During evening and night hours, the traffic volume is much less with a reduced degree of skewness, resulting in lower matching reduction performance.

5.6 Summary

The packet filtering optimization problem has received the attention of the research community for many years. Nevertheless, there is a manifested need for new innovative directions to enable filtering devices such as firewalls to keep up with high-speed networking demands. In this chapter, we first present a taxonomy of dynamic firewall configuration optimization. We believe that this survey can help researchers and engineers to understand the importance of the problem and provide useful guidance for adopting a specific technique based on application requirements.

Second, this chapter presents a new approach for optimizing access control rules based on online traffic statistics, called Dynamic Rule Ordering (DRO). The chapter presents the DRO technique, algorithms and evaluation study to show the effectiveness of DRO. We show that the matching skewness of firewall rules is a profound property to utilize in statistical packet matching. We use this property to optimize the ordering of filtering rules such that it adapts to the current traffic conditions with minimal processing overhead. We consider two factors to determine the importance of a rule in the rule ordering algorithm: rule frequency and recency, which reflect the number and time of rule matching, respectively. We also show how these quantities are calculated from the network traffic statistics with minimal computational and space overhead. The space complexity of our algorithm is bounded by $O(n)$, and the computational complexity is shown to be $O(n^2)$. We can argue that using statistical optimization of firewall rule lists guarantees obtaining minimal average matching time if the traffic statistics get stable over time. Our evaluation of the proposed approach using Internet traffic traces shows that our technique achieves 60 % average matching reduction during day hours, when high performance is crucially needed. We also developed an adaptive mechanism to update the rule list dynamically and keep the matching performance close to optimal with minimum packet matching interruption (about 2–5 times/h). The implementation of our mechanism is simple, lightweight and introduces minimal processing overhead on the standard packet filter processing.

References

1. Adel El-Atawy, Taghrid Samak, Ehab Al-Shaer, and Hong Li. Using online traffic statistical matching for optimizing packet filtering performance. In *INFOCOM'07*, pages 866–874, 2007.
2. Adel El-Atawy, Ehab Al-Shaer, Tung Tran, and Raouf Boutaba. Adaptive early packet filtering for defending firewalls against DoS attacks. In *INFOCOM'09. Rio de Janeiro, Brazil*, pages 2437–2445. IEEE, 2009.
3. E. Al-Shaer and H. Hamed. Modeling and management of firewall policies. *IEEE Transactions on Network and Service Management*, 1(1):2–10, April 2004.
4. D. Bertsimas and J. Tsitsiklis. *Introduction to Linear Optimization*. Athena Scientific, 1997.
5. D. Chapman and E. Zwicky. *Building Internet Firewalls*. Orielly & Associates Inc., second edition, 2000.
6. Cisco Systems. Optimizing ACLs. User Guide for ACL Manager 1.4, CiscoWorks2000, 2002.
7. Cisco Systems. Netflow services solutions guide, October 2004.
8. E. Cohen and C. Lund. Packet classification in large ISPs: Design and evaluation of decision tree classifiers. *ACM SIGMETRICS Performance Evaluation Review*, 33(1):73–84, 2005.
9. Ehab Al-Shaer, Will Marrero, and Adle El-Atawy. Network configuration in a box: Towards end-to-end verification of network reachability and security. In *IEEE International Conference of Network Protocols (ICNP'2009)*, Oct. 2009.
10. Fabio Soldo, Athina Markopoulou, and Katerina J. Argyraki. Optimal filtering of source address prefixes: Models and algorithms. In *IEEE INFOCOM'09*, pages 2446–2454, 2009.
11. R. Graham, E. Lawler, J. Lenstra, and A. Kan. Optimization and approximation in deterministic seuquencing and scheduling: A survey. *Annals of Discrete Mathematics*, 5:287–326, 1979.
12. P. Gupta and N. McKeown. Algorithms for packet classification. *IEEE Network*, 15(2):24–32, 2001.
13. P. Gupta, B. Prabhakar, and S. Boyd. Near optimal routing lookups with bounded worst case performance. In *IEEE INFOCOM'00*, pages 1184–1192, 2000.
14. H. Hamed and E. Al-Shaer. Dynamic rule ordering optimization for high-speed firewall filtering. In *ASIACCS'06*, 2006.
15. H. Hamed and E. Al-Shaer. Dynamic rule-ordering optimization for high-speed firewall filtering. In *ACM AsiaCCS'06*, Mar. 2006.

16. H. Hamed, A. El-Atawy, and E. Al-Shaer. Adaptive statistical optimization techniques for firewall packet filtering. Technical Report CTI-TR-05-012, DePaul University, 2005.
17. H. Hamed, A. El-Atawy, and E. Al-Shaer. Adaptive statistical optimization techniques for firewall packet filtering. In *IEEE INFOCOM'06*, April 2006.
18. D. Knuth. *Fundamental Algorithms*, volume 1 of *The Art of Computer Programming*. Addison-Wesley, Reading, Massachusetts, third edition.
19. K. Lan and J. Heidemann. On the correlation of internet flow characteristics. Technical Report ISI-TR-574, USC/ISI, 2003.
20. E. Lawler. Sequencing jobs to minimize total weighted completion time subject to precedence constraints. *Annals of Discrete Mathematics*, 2:75–90, 1978.
21. J. Lenstra and A. Kan. Complexity of scheduling under precedence constraints. *Operations Research*, 26(1), 1978.
22. D. MacKay. *Information Theory, Inference, and Learning Algorithms*. University of Cambridge, second edition, 2003.
23. Passive Measurement and Analysis Project, National Laboratory for Applied Network Research. Auckland-VIII Traces. http://pma.nlanr.net/Special/auck8.html, December 2003.
24. R. Rivest. On self-organizing sequential search heuristics. *Communications of the ACM*, 19(2):63–67, 1976.
25. A. Schulz. Scheduling to minimize total weighted completion time: Performance guarantees of LP-based heuristics and lower bounds. In *The 5th International IPCO Conference*, pages 301–315, 1996.
26. SimJava v2.0. Process based discrete event simulation package for java. http://www.dcs.ed.ac.uk/home/hase/simjava/, 2002.
27. Subrata Acharya, Jia Wang, Zihui Ge, Taieb F. Znati, and Albert Greenberg. Traffic-aware firewall optimization strategies. In *IEEE International Conference on Communications (ICC) 2006*. IEEE, 2006.
28. D. Taylor and J. Turner. Scalable packet classification using distributed crossproducting of field labels. In *IEEE INFOCOM*, pages 1–12, 2005.
29. J. Wallerich, H. Dreger, A. Feldmann, B. Krishnamurthy, and W. Willinger. A methodology for studying persistency aspects of internet flows. volume 35, pages 23–36, 2005.
30. A. Wool. A quantitative study of firewall configuration errors. *IEEE Computer*, 37(6):62–67, 2004.
31. L. Zhang. Virtual clock: a new traffic control algorithm for packet switching networks. In *The ACM symposium on Communications Architectures and Protocols*, pages 101–124, 1990.
32. G. Zipf. *Human Behaviour and the Principle of Least-Effort*. Addison-Wesley, 1949.

Index

© Springer International Publishing Switzerland 2014
E. Al-Shaer, *Automated Firewall Analytics: Design, Configuration and Optimization*, DOI 10.1007/978-3-319-10371-6

Printed in the United States
By Bookmasters